Fighting Gliders
of World War II

Also by James E. Mrazek

THE ART OF WINNING WARS

THE FALL OF EBEN EMAEL

SAILPLANES AND SOARING

THE GLIDER WAR

HANG GLIDING AND SOARING

Forthcoming

GLIDER ATTACK!

Fighting Gliders of World War II

JAMES E. MRAZEK

author of *The Glider War*

ROBERT HALE LIMITED · LONDON

ST. MARTIN'S PRESS · NEW YORK

© *James E. Mrazek 1977*
First published in Great Britain 1977
First published in the United States of America 1977

Robert Hale Limited
Clerkenwell House
Clerkenwell Green
London EC1R 0HT

ISBN 0 7091 5083 0

St. Martin's Press, Inc.
175 Fifth Avenue
New York, N.Y. 10010

Library of Congress Catalog Card Number 76-57799

ISBN 0 312 28927 8

CONTENTS

ILLUSTRATIONS

ACKNOWLEDGEMENTS————————————

I am indebted to many people for their contributions and for their assistance in preparing this exhaustive (and exhausting) work. Ever since I served as a gliderman during World War II where I collected some of the first data about transport gliders, I have gradually compiled material from many sources and had the help of many people. I trust that I have not omitted attributing contributions from any person or source whatsoever, but if I have inadvertently done so, it has not been intentional.

Regrettably some German material I had used in the manuscript was lost when I mailed it to the U.S. from England where I had been working with the publisher. The data from the material had already been used, but the names of individuals and archives in Germany who had so generously provided the information were recorded in the correspondence lost with the material. Thus I may not have given credit to those sources.

UNITED STATES

N. J. Anthony, for compiling the index

Captain R. S. Barnaby, U.S.N. Ret., test pilot; Commanding Officer, Naval Air Modification Unit, Johnsonville, Pennsylvania

Richard M. Bueschel, author and Japanese and Chinese aviation historian

Eleanor M. Burdette, reference librarian, National Aeronautics and Space Administration (NASA) headquarters library, Washington, D.C.

Colonel Carl F. Damberg, U.S.A.F., wartime chief, Aircraft Laboratory, Wright Field, Ohio

Major Fred Demousse, U.S.A., linguist who assisted in translating of Russian material

The late Major General Frederick R. Dent, U.S.A.F., wartime chief, Glider Branch, Wright Field, Ohio

Marcia Frances, U.S. resident of Vienna, Austria, who translated German material

René Francillon, PhD., author of *Japanese Aircraft*

Royal Frey, Curator, U.S.A.F. Museum, Wright-Patterson Air Force Base, Ohio

Virginia G. Fincik, archives technician, 1361st Photo Squadron, Aerospace Audio Visual Service, U.S.A.F.

Elsie L. T. Goins, office of Naval Aviation History

Jane S. Hess, head, General Reference and Cataloguing, NASA Langley Research Center Library, Hampton, Virginia

Chief Warrant Off. Michael Lansing, U.S.A., German linguist, assisted in translating German materials

Lieutenant Colonel Robert C. Mikesh, U.S.A.F. Ret., assistant curator, aeronautics, also Louis S. Casey, curator of aircraft, National Air and Space Museum, Smithsonian Institution, Washington, D.C.

Rose F. Mrazek, author's mother, translator of Czech material

Lieutenant Colonel Dan Harris, U.S.A. Ret., Japanese linguist

Thomas E. Holman, archivist, Military Archives Branch, National Archives, Washington, D.C.

Thomas Kliment, artist, who did some of the silhouettes

Key K. Kobayashi, assistant head, Japanese Section, Orientalia Division, Library of Congress, Washington, D.C.

Herbert Naylor, linguist, helpful with German and Czech translation.

Rudolf Opitz, wartime *Luftwaffe* assault/transport glider pilot residing in Stamford, Conn.

J. C. Parker, president, Northwestern Aeronautical Corporation, Minneapolis, Minn. during World War II; partner, Auchincloss, Parker and Redpath

Colonel Robert Rentz, U.S.A.F. Ret., wartime transport aircraft pilot

Michael Rosen, historian

Max Rosenberg, Deputy Chief of History; Carl Burger, Chief, Histories Division; David Schoen, Chief, Support Division; Mary Ann Cresswell, archivist; Office of U.S.A.F. History, Washington, D.C.

Lloyd Santmyer, wartime test pilot

Albert F. Simpson, Historical Research Center, Maxwell AF Base, Alabama

Michael Stroukoff, Jr., son of the designer of XCG-14, -14A and the XCG-20

Colonel Floyd J. Sweet, U.S.A.F. Ret., NASA Headquarters, Washington, D.C., wartime commanding officer for a period, AAF Training Detachment, Twenty-nine Palms, Cal. and later glider project officer and test pilot then Chief, Glider Branch, Wright Field, Dayton, Ohio

Major General Louis A. Walsh, U.S.A. Ret., contributor, information on Japanese transport gliders

Paul L. White, archives technician, National Archives

Arthur A. Whiting, wartime aeronautical engineer for Curtis Wright Aircraft Corporation

Robert Vilseck, artist for *National Geographic Magazine* who did portion of glider silhouettes

Woldemar Voigt, wartime head of configuration design and aerodynamics, Messerschmitt, Ltd.

Robert Wolfe, Chief, Captured Records Branch, Military Archives Division, National Archives; also George Wagner, reference specialist, same office.

GERMANY

Edmund Auer, *Luftwaffe* test pilot, engineer

D. C. Consbruch, *Zentralstelle für Luftfahrtdokumentation unde Information ZLDI*

Hans Karl Becker, wartime assault, transport glider pilot

Heiner Lange, *Luftwaffe* assault, transport glider pilot

Alexander Lippisch, aeronautical engineer, pioneer German aircraft designer

H. J. Meier; W. A. Thurow, *Vereinigte Flugtechnische Werke GMBH*

Eugen Moser, *Luftwaffe* assault, transport glider pilot

Dr Sack, *Zentralbibliotek der Bundeswher Der Leiter*

Hanna Reitsch, wartime *Luftwaffe* test pilot

Dr Friedrich Stahl, *Bundesarchiv-Abt. Militararchiv, Freiburg*

Generaloberst Kurt Student, *Luftwaffe*, pioneer in the use of the glider as a military weapon

Diplom Eng. Heinz Trautwein

Oberstleutnant i.G Volker, *Militargeschichtliches Forschungsamt*, Freiburg

also

Messerschmitt-Bolkow-Blohm, and *Hamburger Flugzeugbau GMBH ein inter-nehmensberger der Messerschmitt; Heinkel Flugzeugbau, Vereinigte Flugzeug Werke VFW*, Speyer

BRITAIN

Jean Alexander, author *Russian Aircraft Since 1940*

Jack Beaumont, aviation authority, proprietor Beaumont Aviation Literature

J. M. Bruce, Deputy Keeper, aircraft collection, R.A.F. Museum

Brigadier George Chatterton, author *Wings of Pegasus*, wartime commander Glider Pilot Regiment

Edmund Creek, collector German aircraft data, collaborator on several works on aircraft

Colour-Sergeant T. Fitch, Airborne Forces Museum, Aldershot

J. S. Lucas, Senior Museum Assistant, Photographic Library, Imperial War Museum to whom I am deeply indebted

E. A. Mundey, historian, R.A.F. Archives

Major G. G. Norton, Honorary Curator, Airborne Forces Museum, Aldershot

Lieutenant-Colonel Terence B. H. Otway, D.S.O., wartime commander of 9th Battalion the Parachute Regiment

C. W. Prower, co-ordinating engineer, Hawker-Siddeley Aviation Ltd., formerly on the staff of General Aircraft

Anne Tilbury, archivist, photo collection, *Flight* International

The late Hessel Tiltman, head of team that designed the Horsa glider

W. J. P. Wigmore, general secretary, Glider Pilot Regiment Association

K. G. Wilkinson, Managing Director, Mainline, BEA

also

Public Archives

AUSTRALIA

Warrant Officer A. H. McAulay, Australian Army, historian and sailplane pilot

W. A. Smither, Department of Air, Canberra

CANADA

S. F. Wise, Director, Directorate of History, Department of National Defence,
   Ottawa

FRANCE

M. Henri Michel, *Directeur de recherche au Centre national de la recherche scientifique*
Raymond Danel, aeronautical engineer, historian

INDIA

Squadron Leader B. S. Hatangade, Assistant Air Attaché, Indian Embassy,
   Washington, D.C.

ITALY

Ing. Angelo Ambrosini, designer and builder of transport glider AL-12P
Colonel S. SM Vittoria Castiglioni, Army Office of Military History

JAPAN

Lieutenant Colonel Hideo Aoki
Ikuhiko Hata, Chief Historian, Ministry of Finance, Tokyo
Commander Sadao Seno
Yoshisuke Yamaguchi

SWEDEN

Rudolf Abelin, aircraft designer and test pilot, president and general manager
   of Saab-Scania, Malmo
Kjell Lagerstrom, SAAB, New York

PICTURE CREDITS

U.S. Air Force: 1, 46, 73, 74, 75, 78, 80, 81, 84, 87, 89, 92, 96, 97, 101, 103, 104, 107, 112, 115, 116, 119, 130
Fritz Stamer: 5
Institut für Flugausrüstung: 6
U.S. Air Force in U.S. National Archives: 9, 36
Wright Field Collection in U.S. National Archives: 10
E. J. Creek: 11, 13, 23, 24
Bundesarchiv: 14
Smithsonian Institution: 16, 21, 42, 51, 76, 79, 90, 93, 102, 106, 109, 110, 113, 120, 128, 144, 149
Messerschmidt Archives: 18
Hamburger Flugzeugbau (GmbH): 31, 32
Flight: 38, 45, 136
Planet News: 39
Imperial War Museum: 43, 47, 48, 49, 52, 53, 56
Luftfahrtarchiv: 61
Navy Department in U.S. National Archives: 64, 66
U.S. Army: 65, 129, 131
Roger W. Griswold: 82
William K. Horn: 85
U.S. National Archives: 86
M. B. Passingham: 139
J. P. Alexander: 142, 147
Royal Australian Air Force: 145
Peter Selinger: 157
Giorgio Evangelisti: 157
Skane-Reportage: 158
Air Enthusiast: 160, 161

To My Wife, Thelma

ONE

Fighting Gliders—
the Secret Weapon

This compact volume tells the heretofore little-known technical facts about the assault and transport gliders that so heroically served the fighting forces of Germany, Great Britain, Soviet Union and America during World War II. It also reveals for the first time little-known facts about the gliders other nations produced.

Not before or since that cataclysmic conflict has the world used the glider in war. The appearance of this aircraft in war was destined to be but once. Technological shortcomings, production, supply and delivery problems, and less than far-sighted military leadership, combined to prevent its potential from becoming fully realised before the end of the war swept this formidable weapon from history's stage.

The glider introduced the world to a new kind of airborne warfare. On 10 May 1940 ten German gliders carrying seventy-eight glidermen assaulted the enormous Fort Eben Emael, pride of the Allied defences. Twenty-five minutes later the fort and its 750 defenders had been rendered ineffective for the rest of the war by the audacious glidermen's attack. This led to tremendous interest in the military glider in Great Britain, Japan and the United States. Later the Allies used gliders in Normandy, Arnhem, Wesel and a forgotten jungle strip in Burma—to list but a few of the glider's stirring feats.

Few realise that America produced 14,000 combat gliders—more than any type of its famed fighter or bomber aeroplanes, with the possible exception of one or two fighter models. At one time America planned to build 36,000 gliders, and training was scheduled for more than that number of glider pilots, for the indomitable glider armada that might have swarmed over and inundated the Third Reich.

What advantages did gliders have that made them a useful weapon in combat, and a desirable cargo air-transport vehicle? There were many. Gliders gave mobility to ground units. Using gliders, forces could leap rivers, mountains and enemy defences to make vertical envelopment possible. Armies could operate in a third dimension. Gliders made airborne warfare not only a possibility but a reality.

Gliders could carry a squad, a platoon or a company in a single load. They discharged units ready to fight, not scattered over a landscape, in the way paratroopers landed.

Gliders were also cheap to manufacture, in contrast to the cost of an aeroplane. According to the number of gliders an aeroplane towed, they could double or triple the amount of men or cargo a single plane could move through the air.

Most important of all, the glider was silent. Stealth was its trademark, and the terror it spread was a psychological advantage of unsurpassed importance.

Fighting gliders were a breed apart, different from any aircraft theretofore known. Their forerunner, the sailplane or sports glider, could use winds and thermal currents efficiently in 'sail flight', and remain aloft for hours and travel many miles.

Sailplanes differed considerably from war gliders. Sailplanes have long, narrow wings and a pencil-like fuselage; they appear almost translucent against the sky and sun and manoeuvre gracefully with swallow-like convolutions. Gliders have stubbier wings, large bodies, and most of them look much like an aeroplane without an engine.

Unlike the sports glider, the fighting, transport, cargo, assault or combat glider could not use atmospheric thermals to remain aloft. Once a military glider was released, and its speed diminished to a critical point, its weight, design, and construction prevented it from obtaining lift from air currents or thermals to keep it up, and it began to glide down to the earth. Most of the craft produced during World War II had about a one to ten glide ratio; that is, in free flight they glided down at the rate of one foot for every ten feet they flew forward. At that period the sailplane had a one to twenty ratio. (Today sailplanes are being built that have as much as a one to fifty ratio, so great have been the technological advances since the war.)

To get into the air, the sports glider was towed by aeroplane or auto until it got up enough speed to lift it off the ground; or it could be rolled down a slope to get enough speed to take off, or 'winched' into the air, shooting like a missile from a slingshot to gain enough speed to fly.

The combat glider had to be towed off the ground behind a powerful aeroplane, or later, 'snatched' from the ground by an aeroplane in flight. A long rope, usually of nylon, stretched from the nose or wings of the glider to the tail of the aeroplane. The glider was towed all the way to a point just short of, or above, its target. In many airborne assaults in World War II gliders flew behind tow-planes in 'serials' of planes and gliders that stretched out in the sky for hundreds of miles, an awe-inspiring sight to front-line troops over whose heads they flew.

Once on their mission, gliders flew through rough weather and sheets of flak. Those that survived the trip unhitched above the enemy and glided down into battle. There was no escape on the winds, the commitment was irrevocable. Once a plane and glider took off with a cargo, or glidermen, or tank, only the aeroplane returned.

Glider flight serial skims the landscape. Waco CG-4A gliders in double tow behind Curtis Commando C-46s

TWO

German Gliders

The development of Germany's military transport gliders dates from the early 1930s. Interest sprouted from a widespread national enthusiasm for sports gliding and soaring; an outcome of the restrictions imposed on Germany on the development and production of powered aircraft by the World War I Treaty of Versailles, signed in 1919.

As a result of the treaty, the energies of a nation noted for a strong interest in aviation, evidenced by the production of Fokker and other fighter aeroplanes and of dirigibles, were now restrictively channelled into gliding and soaring, the only outlet remaining for aviation enthusiasts. German achievements in gliding and soaring laid the foundation for Germany's later air power.

By 1932 something new was taking place; the Germans were visualising potential in the frail sailplane as other than a recreational air vehicle. While the earlier gliders and sailplanes had been slung or thrust into thermals, to gain their pilots a few moments of exhilarating pleasure in the air, now planes were towing gliders for hundreds of miles; pilots were also learning to tow two or more (in fact a train of gliders) behind a single plane. (Someone in America had also delivered mail by glider.)

By 1932 the Germans had also produced a glider large enough to carry meteorological equipment, a pilot and one or two scientists to man the equipment and conduct meteorological tests.

This glider was designed by Dr Alexander Lippisch in collaboration with Professor Walter Georgii at the Rhoen-Rossiten-Gesellschaft Research Institute in Munich. The actual construction of the glider took place in the workshop of Alex Schleicher in Poppenhausen.

For meteorological readings at high altitudes this glider was ideal. When released it was noiseless, vibrationless and free from electrical emanations usually found in aeroplanes that was likely to disturb sensitive instruments. The 'flying observatory' (OBS), as it became known, flew many research flights.

According to the *Air Enthusiast* (March 1972) Adolf Hitler took an interest in the OBS in Munich when he went to visit an exhibition at the airport. At that time he conferred with Professor Georgii and discussed the possibility of still larger gliders for military transport tasks.

How closely the Germans followed Soviet glider development is not precisely known. The few published facts are revealing and significant, however. For years before the Germans developed their 'flying observatory' glider, the forerunner of their transport glider the DFS 230, German and Soviet military collaboration had been a matter of historical fact. General Kurt Student, who later headed the Nazi airborne forces during the war, and was the highest ranking proponent of glider warfare in the armies of the world (at that time he was a captain) visited the Lipetsk airfield, a German base in Russia, in the years 1924 to 1928. It is also known that General Ernst Udet, the German World War I fighter ace, visited Russia many times. That Student and other high-ranking officers gleaned data about Soviet glider activities is virtually certain.

Udet was involved in the German glider research and development programme from its inception. It was he, according to William Green in his *Warplanes of the Third Reich* who suggested that the flying observatory should be modified to carry soldiers. Along with General Udet, some of the more visionary members of the Air Forces, General Jeschonnek in particular, began to press for a combat model. The design and development of the project was given a 'secret' classification right at the start and was turned over to the Deutsche Forschungsantalt Fuer Segelflug (DFS), an affiliate to the Rhoen Research Institute. An aircraft engineer, Hans Jacobs, assisted by glider pilots on the staff of the company, took the problem in hand. Green who is a leading authority on world aircraft states that the DFS 230, a successor to the flying observatory, '. . . began flight tests late in 1937. Assuming Mr. Green to be correct, the Germans were at least two years, and perhaps as much as four years, behind the Russians in developing a transport glider as such.

Where the Germans may have been first, and this point is debatable, is in conceiving of the glider not as just an air transport vehicle for military or commercial cargo or passenger use, but as an attack weapon. This concept was either General Udet's or General Student's. Udet thought of the glider as the modern equivalent of the Trojan Horse, landing soldiers in stealth and silence behind enemy lines. Student's approach was more aggressive—he saw gliders as a direct attacking and fighting weapon. He was to see his theory vindicated when Hitler ordered him to capture the Belgian fort, Eben Emael, in the opening attack on the West in May 1940. Eleven gliders carrying seventy-eight glidermen landed on the world's most 'impregnable' fort, and within twenty minutes neutralised its 780-man garrison. The next day the fort capitulated. With this feat glider warfare was born.

The Germans rated all their gliders as combat aircraft. Germany was the only country to arm every glider with machine guns. The DFS 230 carried one, the Go 242 eight, and the Me 321 two or more. Thus in Germany gliders were definitely considered to be fighting

'OBS', meteorological observation glider, forerunner of German military attack and transport gliders

DFS 230 attack glider. In history's first airborne assault, seventy-eight German glider troops in ten DFS 230s attacked and captured Belgian Fort Eben Emael, 10th May 1940

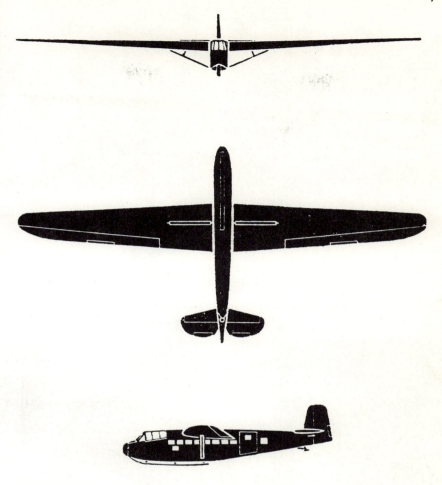

DFS 230, three-view section

aircraft, whereas other nations considered them rather as military transports. Later the other nations took advantage of German experience, and used gliders operationally in much the same way as the Germans had done.

DFS 230

The DFS 230 was an outgrowth of an earlier transport glider built by the Rhoen-Rositten-Gesellschaft Research Institute in the early 1930s as a 'flying observatory', to carry meteorological instruments.

DFS 230 and Bf 109 Mistelschlepp (pick-a-back) combination

DFS 230 laden with electronic components, illustrating one of the many purposes for which German gliders were used. This DFS was one element of an experimental airborne communications system

The DFS 230 was designed by Hans Jacobs, Chief Engineer at the Institute. It was first tested by Hanna Reitsch, the famous, diminutive, German aviatrix—who also test-piloted the V bombs which later rained on Britain.

The wings of the glider were set high, and braced. The fuselage was a framework of steel tubing covered with fabric with a rectangular cross section. The wings were of stressed plywood with spoilers fitted on the upper surface to steepen the angle of glide. The wheels could be jettisoned; the glider then landed on a single central ski that extended from the nose to about the middle of its belly.

The DFS 230 was flown by one pilot and carried nine troops. The seats in the first model were in a straight line, six facing forward, four to the rear. The rear seats could be taken out to allow for cargo. The glider weighed 1,800 pounds and could carry up to 2,800 pounds of cargo. It had a wing-span of 72 feet, and was 37.5 feet long. It was normally towed at 120 miles per hour.

The Initial model was later modified. Loading doors had to be changed to accommodate a greater variety of loads, such as bicycles, anti-tank guns and motor-cycles.

A light machine-gun was fixed externally to the starboard side, and manned by the occupant of the second seat who fired through a slit in the fuselage. A later model had the machine gun just aft of the canopy. Navigation lights were operated by a generator fixed to the nose of the glider. Clamps along the seats held carbines and machine pistols.

Large-scale production was launched under the supervision of the Gotha works. Many different companies ultimately participated in the production endeavour, including the Hartwig Toy Factory, at Sonnenberg in Thuringia. In all, 2,230 DFS 230's were built.

Models B-1 and B-2 had dual controls and could carry more weight. Designers also incorporated braking rockets and parachutes for deceleration in landing.

This glider was used to open the German invasion of the West, in the assault on Fort Eben Emael. It was used in the invasion of Crete, and flew urgently-needed men and supplies to General Rommel's Africa Corps. Later, valiant efforts were made to get supplies to German Armies fighting in Russia by DFS 230, and it also stood by to participate in a gigantic, desperate, last-minute attempt to launch an airborne assault against the Russian forces at Stalingrad.

DFS-230s were fitted out as work shops containing lathes, other machine tools, welding equipment and cabinets with an assortment of spare parts for fighter and other combat aeroplanes. One squadron of each fighter group on the Eastern Front towed these fighter maintenance and repair gliders to each base from which the group operated so that the group had immediate maintenance facilities available.

Technical Data

Glider Model: DFS 230
Type: assault glider
Crew: pilot
Dimensions
    Wing-span: 72ft
    Wing area: 444sq ft
    Fuselage
      Length: 37.5ft
    Cargo compartment
      Length: 13.2ft
      Width: 3.6ft
      Height: 4.5ft

Weight
    Total with cargo: 4,600lb
    Empty: 1,800lb
    Cargo: 2,800lb
Loadings
    Nine troops, equipped, or
    equivalent in cargo
Armament
    In some adaptations a
    machine gun
Flight performance
    Towing speed: 120mph

Tow-planes: He 111, He 126, Ju 52/53, Ju 87, Bf 110

DFS-230 V7

A DFS 230 V7 was also developed. As William Green explains so aptly in *Warplanes of the Third Reich*, it '. . . bore no relationship to the basic DFS 230 design', the appellation being a way of getting round bureaucratic intransigence so as to permit designers to build a new and better glider than the DFS 230 without raising resentment or objections.

Completed in 1943, it carried fifteen troops (six more than the prototype) or the equivalent weight of 4,180 pounds of cargo. Its cargo compartment was longer, its wing-span less and the length of the fuselage over three feet greater. A novel feature was that a panel on the top was removable to enable loading through the roof.

Despite the fact that the DFS 230 V7 was a marked improvement on the DFS 230 in the weight and number of men it carried, and had many new features, it was not accepted for production.

Technical Data

Glider Model: DFS 230 V7
Type: assault/transport
    glider
Crew: pilot, co-pilot
Dimensions
    Wing-span: 63.6ft
    Wing area: 425sq ft
    Fuselage
      Length: 41ft
    Cargo compartment
      Length: 14.9ft

Weight
    Total with cargo: 7,700lb
    Empty: 3,520lb
    Cargo: 4,180lb
Loadings
    Fifteen troops, equipped.
Armament
    3 machine-guns
Flight performance
    Maximum towing speed:
    180mph

DFS 230 V-7, three-view section

Gotha Go 242 parked at Wright Army Air Field, Ohio. This captured German glider was brought to the United States, assembled and extensively studied and tested

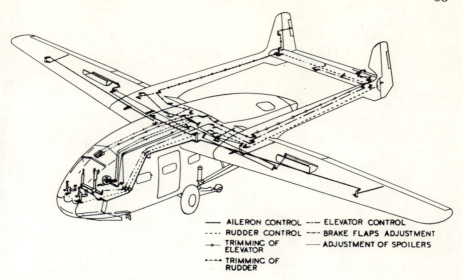

AILERON CONTROL --- ELEVATOR CONTROL
.... RUDDER CONTROL ·-·- BRAKE FLAPS ADJUSTMENT
TRIMMING OF ──── ADJUSTMENT OF SPOILERS
ELEVATOR
TRIMMING OF
RUDDER

Gotha Go 242: (*above*) control system and (*below*) fitted with bank of four Rheinmetall RI 502 solid fuel rockets to assist in take-off

Close-up of RI 502 solid fuel rocket propulsion system

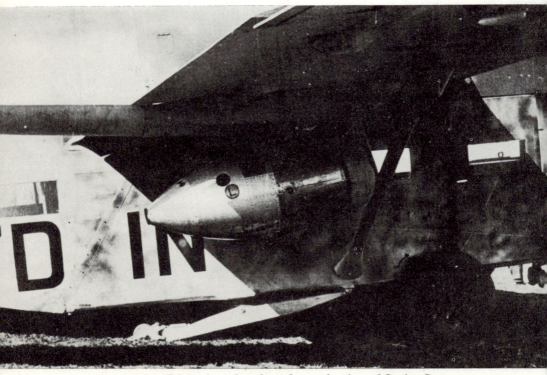

Walter RI 202b rocket slung beneath wing of Gotha Go 242

shops, with lathes and other machinery permanently installed. Others had staff or command operations rooms. They were flown from location to location, as the need arose for their equipment. The chief tow-aircraft for the Go 242 were the He 111Z and the Ju 52. In all, Gothaer and its affiliates built 1,528 Go 242's. One hundred and thirty three Go 242's were modified to become aeroplanes, by the addition of two engines, and became known as the Go 244.

The Go 242 was used extensively for personnel and supply missions between German bases in Europe and North Africa, to supply Rommel's Africa Corps. In Russia they were used to help maintain Wermacht mobility by flying supplies to extended ground force columns. They flew critical supplies to beleagured German forces at Kholm early in 1942, and to the encircled panzer army in Podolsk. They also assisted in evacuating German forces from Crimea.

Me 321

The *Gigant* (Giant), as the Messerschmitt Me 321 was called, was the world's largest operational glider and one of the largest aircraft built until recent years. It had a wing-span of 181 feet, was 93 feet long, and carried 24 tons. It has frequently been confused with the Junkers Ju 322 and called the *Merseburg* after the city of this name where the Ju 322, another enormous German glider, was built.

An urgent requirement for a large glider developed when German military leaders concluded that any airborne assault on England must be backed up by air-landed tanks, self-propelled guns, and the indispensable 88 mm anti-aircraft guns. Without these weapons the invasion of England would be doomed, they felt.

The idea for a large glider for this strategic mission may have originated at Messerschmitt Ltd. According to Mr Woldemar Voigt, who was head of the office of configuration design and aerodynamics at the company, Professor Willy Messerschmitt discussed the feasibility of building such an enormous aircraft with Mr Voigt early in November 1940. Apparently, it was an idea first broached to Mr Messerschmitt a month earlier by Mr Joseph Froelich, a department head. In a matter of days after design studies began, Mr Voigt assured Professor Messerschmitt that it was not only possible to design such a glider, but also to tow it.

Professor Messerschmitt had an audience with Rudolf Hess, the Deputy Fuehrer, and made the proposal to build such an aircraft. Hess went to Adolf Hitler, who, intrigued with the idea, gave the go ahead in a few days. Hess then turned the details over to the Air Ministry.

Mr Voigt went on to produce the configuration design and aerodynamic layout. Mr Froelich was given the mission of implementing

Pkw personnel carr
being loaded into
a Gotha Go 242

Messerschmitt Me 321, largest glider ever built, compare Go 242 beneath wing

Messerschmitt Me
321, showing
interior

the concept. He set up a sizable task force of engineers and assorted supporting skills at Leipheim to initiate the construction. Meanwhile, the Air Ministry issued a production order. Assembly of the gliders took place at Leipheim and Obertraubling. The first test flight was made at Leipheim on 25 February 1941, about fifteen weeks after the construction order had been given.

Flight tests were first carried out without loads, the glider being towed by a Junkers (Ju) 90, the only aircraft powerful enough to get the *Gigant* into the air. It took 4,000 feet of runway to get the wheels off the ground; the Germans encountered extreme difficulty in getting the glider airborne when it carried a load. Since they had few aeroplanes as powerful as the Ju 90, and it was evident that this plane was not powerful enough to tow a fully-loaded Me 321, they resorted to the 'Troika tow,' a Messerschmitt concept, which was a combination of three towing aircraft each independently hitched to the glider by a tow-rope. The Troika tow proved successful. The aeroplanes used for this purpose were the Bf 110c fighter-bomber, or the Me 110.

Ultimately, the Troika tow became costly in aircraft and pilots lost in experimentation, and in the number of aircraft that it took from critical operations, so a special tug, the He 111Z was built. The product of the imagination of General Ernst Udet, it consisted of two He 111 H-6 twin-engine bombers, attached by a constant-chord wing section with an engine mounted at the centre, making the five-engine He 111Z which became known as the *Zwilling*. Full controls were in the port side fuselage. The second pilot sat in the other fuselage and had full controls but no throttles. The total crew was five. It had a wing span of 116 feet.

At take-off with maximum load eight auxiliary rockets were used to assist the tow-plane. Each of 1,200 pounds thrust, they were suspended from the lower surface of the *Gigant's* wings. When expended, the rockets were dropped by parachute. Landing gear could be dropped, and landing accomplished on four spring skids.

The fuselage was made of steel tubing covered with fabric. Wings were made of steel tubes giving a rectangular cross section and interconnected, as in a girder structure. Plywood covered the wing forward of the spar. Fabric covered the wing aft of the spar.

Once airborne, the *Gigant* handled well but proved a tremendous physical strain for one pilot to fly. This caused the designers to modify the glider to provide for a co-pilot.

Most 321's were first based in France in preparation for a German invasion of Great Britain. When the invasion did not occur, these gliders were transferred to the Russian front, where many of them were used to fly men, materials and equipment. The glider carried 200 fully equipped men. When it carried troops, the storage space was

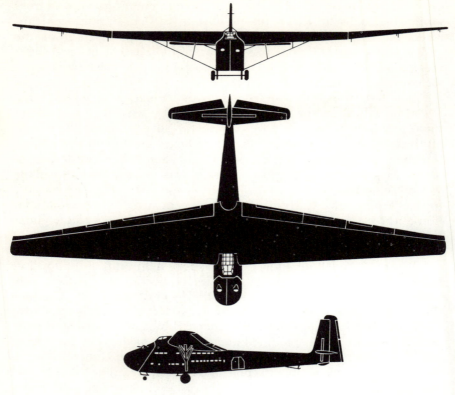

Messerschmitt Me 321, three-view section

Technical Data

Glider Model: Me 321
Type: assault transport glider
Crew: pilot, co-pilot,
   mechanic
Dimensions
   Wing-span: 181ft
   Wing area: 3,230sq ft
   Fuselage
     Length: 93ft
     Height: 19ft
Weight
   Total with cargo: 70,000lb
   Empty: 26,000lb
   Cargo: 44,000lb

Loadings
   Heavy tank; or an 88 mm
   anti-tank gun and prime
   mover; or 200 troops,
   equipped.
Armament
   Several machine guns
Flight performance
   Maximum airspeed:
   110mph
Tow-planes: Ju 90, three Me 110's,
   or one He 111Z

Messerschmitt Me 321 in tow behind five-engined Heinkel He 111Z

Heinkel 111Z

divided into an upper and a lower compartment, to carry a full company of men and their equipment.

Two hundred of these immense gliders were built. As the war progressed, a large number were converted into six-engine Me 323 aeroplanes.

Some aeronauticists and historians doubt the Me 321 could actually carry 200 troops. According to Woldemar Voigt, its designer, there was no question of this capacity, and ability to transport even heavier loads. This was dramatically proven. The heavier Me 323 aeroplane, evacuated 220 men of General Erwin Rommel's forces from North Africa to Italy on at least one flight. Eighty sat in the wings, one hundred and forty in the cargo compartment.

Ju 322

This was the real mystery glider of World War II, and one about which few details are known to this day. It was one of Germany's super gliders, sometimes referred to by the Germans as the *Goliath*, and finally officially named the *Mammut*. British Intelligence dubbed it the *Merseberg* (see Me 321). It had a chequered history.

The belief was long held that Junkers went into the production of the Ju 322 to compete with Messerschmitt's Me 321 and to get a share of the large cargo transport glider market. Actually this was not the case.

The Ju 322 was the result of almost frantic efforts to build tank and heavy equipment carrying gliders for the invasion of England. When the Reich Air Ministry instructed Messerschmitt to design a glider (ultimately the Me 321), it placed the same requirement on Junkers. The only difference in the instructions issued was that Messerschmitt were allowed to use steel; Junkers were to use wood, in anticipation of a critical shortage of steel, in which case the Air Ministry could fall back on Junkers' product to meet future requirements for large cargo gliders.

The Ju 322 was in every sense of the word a 'flying wing', a rare design in aircraft at any period in history. It was absolutely extraordinary that this should have been the basic design for such a huge aircraft; a wing design not at that time thoroughly tested even in the sporting glider, except perhaps by Russia.

The glider was to carry twenty tons of cargo, somewhat less than the amount the Me 321 carried. The wing was 203 feet long of wood throughout except for fittings, instruments and the like. The reinforced middle beam was actually the fuselage. The fuselage part of the wing had a leading edge that could be detached to open the immense interior for cargo. The cockpit was on the left side of the cargo compartment and above it.

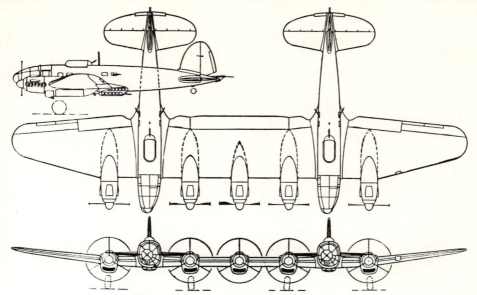

Heinkel He 111Z, three-view section

Messerschmitt Me 323 aeroplane. Although rated for 200 passengers as a glider, on at least one flight, the Me 323 transported 240 men (eighty in the wings, 160 in the fuselage) to Sicily from North Africa despite the added weight of the six engines

Designing and developing the landing gear and undercarriage proved one of the most difficult problems. The glider plus its load weighed close on forty-five tons. Despite the original ruling against its use, eight tons of steel had to go into the construction of the various parts to give them the necessary rigidity and strength.

The undercarriage had to be under the glider as it was being loaded. Then, either the glider had to be towed to flying speed and take off from the undercarriage, letting it coast along the runway, or the undercarriage had to be dropped after take-off. The latter course was decided upon. So heavy was the gear itself, however, that the engineers calculated that it could not be dropped from too great a height or it would be destroyed when it hit the ground. If it was dropped at too low an altitude it would bounce up and hit the glider. Many different kinds of gear were tested, with from eight to as many as thirty-two wheels (sixteen in tandem on each side).

Problems were also encountered with the wooden structure. It was found that because of poor manufacturing techniques parts were weakened by rot. The first tank loaded into the glider fell through the floor. (This was due in part to faulty ramp design.) This incident led to the reinforcement of the floor, whereby the problem of loading future tanks and similarly heavy equipment was solved, but at the expense of useful payload. It took an additional eight tons of material to effect the reinforcement, reducing the payload to fourteen tons. Other changes, and some cautionary calculations, caused the designers to reduce the payload to twelve tons.

In time two prototypes were ready for tests. Even before flight tests began, General Ernst Udet, World War I fighter ace, while visiting Junkers, expressed his doubts that the glider would really fly. Junkers officials were so confident of the outcome of their daring venture, however, that they launched into the construction of ninety-eight more *Mammuts*.

The first test took place in April 1941. Reports state that at full throttle the Ju 90 bomber, which was towing the Ju 322, could not get up enough speed to lift the glider off the runway. In a subsequent try the glider managed to get off the ground but could make no change in direction, and had to cut off from the Ju 90 and land only a short distance from the take-off field. In the test the glider had so little vertical stability that its wings rotated in minor arcs, swinging the tow-plane dangerously.

No other tests were made. Already facing a huge financial loss, and with no assurance the Ju 322 would be successful, Junkers decided to terminate the project. The hulls of the existing prototypes and those under construction were cut up, and the wood obtained was used in automobile gas generators.

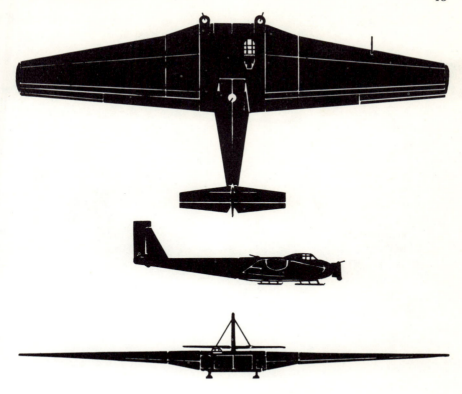

Junkers Ju 322, three-view section

Junkers planned to build a yet larger glider, the Ju-488 at Toulouse, France. However, Allied bombings of Toulouse industrial sites destroyed the factory where the glider was to be built and it was decided to teminate the project.

Technical Data

Glider Model: Ju 322
Type: heavy-cargo glider
Dimensions
  Wing-span: 203ft
  Wing area: 6,400sq ft
  Fuselage
   Length: 95ft
  Cargo compartment
   Length: 38ft
   Width: 30ft
   Height: 10.1ft

Weight
  Total with cargo: 90,000lb
  Empty: 56,000lb
  Cargo: 24,000lb
Loadings
  PzKW IV tank; 100 troops, equipped.
Armament
  Two 7.9-mm machine guns
Tow-planes: Ju 90 V7

Junkers Ju 322

DFS 331

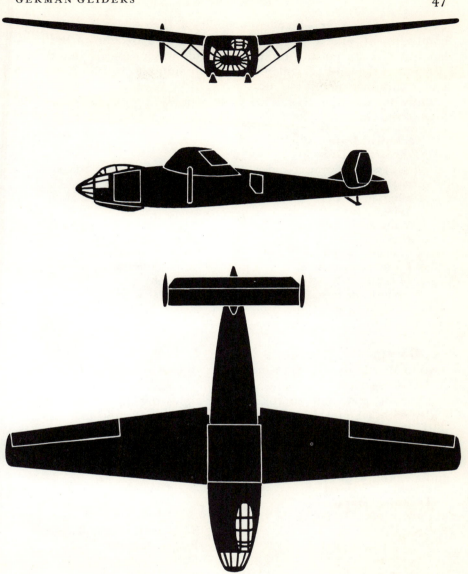

DFS 331, three-view section

DFS 331

This glider was designed by Hans Jacobs, also designer of the DFS 230. It was built by Gothaer Waggonfabrik in 1941; at about the time Gothaer was also proceeding with the design and construction of the Go-242. Although the DFS 331 possessed some features novel to gliders of the time—excellent visibility in the cockpit, a wide cargo compartment, and a superb airfoil longitudinal section of the fuselage—it did not go into production. This was primarily due to the progress of the Go-242, which had equally suitable characteristics and larger cargo capacity.

Only one was built. It carried 4,500 pounds, approximately half the load of the Go 242.

Technical Data

Glider Model: DFS 331
Type: assault/transport glider
Crew: pilot, co-pilot
Dimensions
  Wing-span: 71ft
  Wing area: 646sq ft
  Fuselage
    Length: 51.9ft
  Cargo compartment
    Length: 20ft
    Width: 8.3ft
    Height: 5.3ft

Weight
  Total with cargo: 10,000lb
  Empty: 5,500lb
  Cargo: 4,500lb
Loadings
  Eighteen troops, equipped
  or 4,500lb of cargo.
Flight performance
  Maximum towing speed:
  168mph

Go 345

Two models of the Go 345 were produced by Gothaer Waggonfabrik A. G., of Gotha.

The Go 345A, built in 1944, was a high-wing monoplane assault glider with a high-set braced tail. Both wings and tail-fins had trim tabs. The landing gear was a semi-detachable tricycle gear of simple design. It could be loaded through detachable side doors. The design also permitted rapid exit of troops. The frame was made of steel tubing and covered with plywood.

Technical Data

Glider Model: Go 345A
Type: cargo glider
Crew: pilot, co-pilot
Dimensions
  Wing-span: 67ft
  Wing area: 537sq ft
  Fuselage
    Length: 41.3ft
    Height: 15.5ft
  Cargo compartment
    Length: 13ft
    Width: 4.3ft
    Height: 5.1ft

Weight
  Total with cargo: 8,950lb
  Empty: 5,450lb
  Cargo: 3,500lb
Loadings
  Twelve troops, equipped.

The Go 345A carried a pilot and co-pilot, side by side, and had dual controls. Two Argus-pulse thrusters could be attached, one under each wing; these were designed to be started after the towline was dropped, when the glider had reached its destination, to give the pilot more flight range and thus more option in the choice of landing sites. They also helped him to avoid hostile fire.

A second model, the Go 345B, was built to carry cargo. Instead of side doors it had a short nose which, along with the pilot compartment in it, could be swung up to permit loading. Wheels were used instead of skids. Neither glider was produced in quantity.

Ka 430

This glider was the result of one of the more ambitious tactical designs. It was developed in the summer of 1944 under the auspices of Albert Kalkert, Technical Director of the Reporaturwerke Erfurt aircraft factories, in co-operation with the Gotha design bureau, and it was to have been mass-produced during the winter of 1944–45. Subsequent developments in the war made this impossible.

The Ka 430 was both an assault and a transport glider. It was a high-performance aircraft especially constructed for towing speeds up to 220 miles per hour. It was towable by almost any aircraft, including the Me 109 and the FW 190, and had provision for the use of the *starschlepp*, or non-flexible towing bar, by which it was attached to the tow-plane, or of a 'Y' tow-cable, attached to the forward wing surfaces on either side of the fuselage.

The glider had a composite wood and metal frame construction. It had a tricycle landing gear for landings in prepared areas. If a landing in rugged terrain or an unprepared landing-zone was anticipated, this could be dropped and the glider could land on skids. There was a parachute brake as well as rocket deceleration devices.

Loading could be carried out from the rear, on a ramp formed by dropping a rear portion hinged to the glider. One side of the fuselage had detachable panels that could be taken off for loading or rapid unloading. The glider could carry twelve glidermen. A later modification introduced floor hatchways through which six paratroopers at a time could drop to the ground on a cylindrical platform shaped like a top. The paratroopers sat in seats around the platform, facing inward, attached to their seats by safety belts. The platform was attached to a chute. This concept was never tested, however.

The glider was armed with a machine-gun affixed to a manually-operated gun-turret which protruded forward from the top of the cockpit. It also had an armour-plated cockpit floor to protect the pilots.

A total of twelve Ka 430's were manufactured.

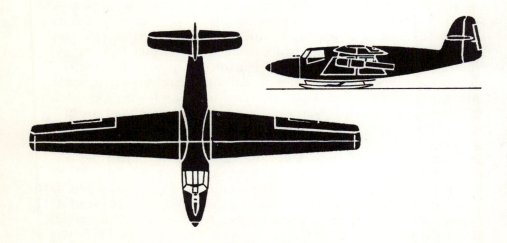

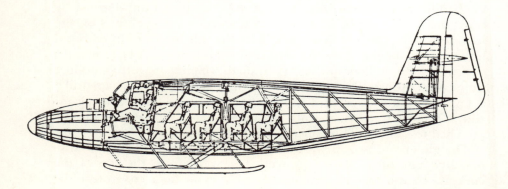

Gotha Go 345A, three-view section and exploded drawing

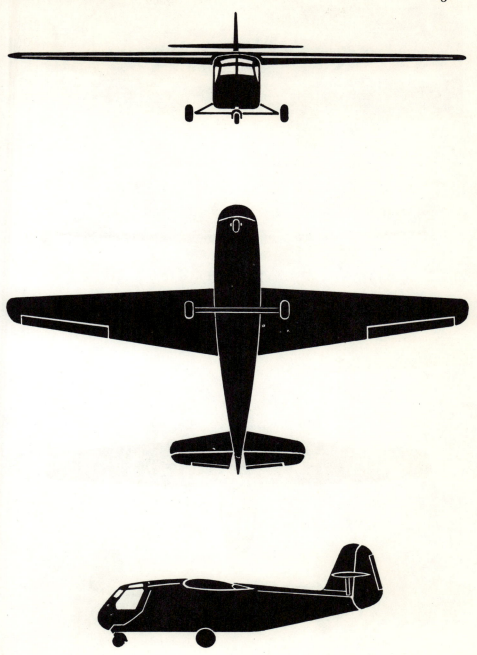

Gotha Go 345B, three-view section

Gotha-Kalkert Ka 430

Gotha-Kalkert Ka 430, three-view section

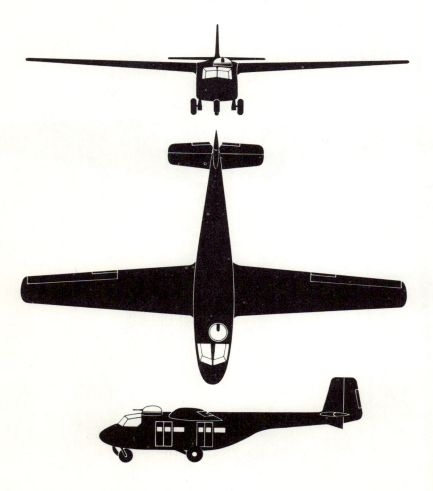

Technical Data

Glider Model: Ka 430
Type: assault and transport
glider
Crew: pilot, co-pilot
Dimensions
Wing-span: 64ft
Wing area: 435sq ft
Fuselage
Length: 44ft
Height: 15ft
Cargo compartment
Length: 12ft
Width: 5.6ft
Height: 5.3ft

Weight
Total with cargo: 7,500lb
Empty: 3,750lb
Cargo: 3,750lb
Loadings
Twelve troops, equipped
either parachute troops or
glidermen; equipment in
lieu of an equivalent weight
of men.
Armament
One machine gun.
Tow-planes: Me 109, FW 190
or slower aircraft

BV 40

As World War II progressed, Allied bombers became more difficult for the German Luftwaffe to cope with. The Luftwaffe leaders were frantically searching for a method to counter the tightly-knit Allied B-17 formations flying almost untouched by German fighters. Dr. Richard Vogt, chief designer and technical director of Blohm and Voss, proposed the idea of an unpowered glider—a 'glide-fighter'— to intercept them, to the German Air Ministry. The idea was that a fighter should tow the interceptor to a height well above the bomber formations and release it when bombers came within glider range, letting the glider swoop into the Allied bombers. Its head-on attack would be so fast that it would be invisible to a bomber's gunner until the glider pilot had fired his 30-mm cannon and had vanished.

The Reich Air Ministry thought Dr Vogt's proposal worth exploring, and Blohm and Voss was given an order for the BV 40, which was to become the world's only interceptor glider.

It was a remarkably small glider with a wing span of 25.96 feet, and a length of 18.7 feet. The pilot lay down flat on padded mats, his chin resting on a short padded post, in a compartment of welded sheet steel armour plate, the front panel more than 20 mm thick; the windshield was made of 120 mm non-fragmenting glass. Two steel panels could be slid forward overhead to give additional protection. The armament consisted of two 30 mm MK 108 cannons.

The glider was towed by a BF 109G. It took off on a two-wheeled trolley, the trolley being jettisoned as soon as the craft was airborne. It landed on skids. It was flight-tested in late May 1944, and over a period of several months thereafter several models were produced.

There were many different concepts as to the glider's usage. Pulse

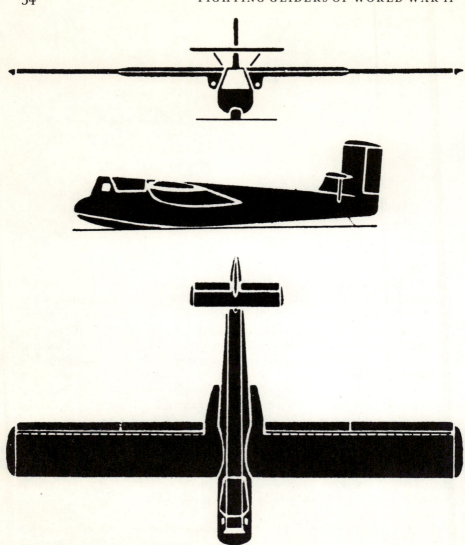

Blom Voss BV 40, three-view section

jets and rockets for emergency thrust were considered. It was suggested that it should carry small bombs to be dropped on enemy formations, or be made into a towed fuel tank, or that it should be used as a bomb-glider releasable from the wing of a large bomber.

Tests showed it could dive at speeds of 292 miles per hour, and it was felt that a 560 mile per hour speed could be attainable. Nineteen prototypes were produced.

Blom Voss interceptor glider BV 40. The pilot flew lying prone

Blom Voss BV 40

Technical Data

Glider Model: BV 40

Type: interceptor-glider

Crew: pilot

Dimensions
  Wing-span: 25.96ft
  Wing area: 93.6sq ft
  Fuselage
    Length: 18.7ft

Weight
  Total with cargo: 2,094lb
  Empty: 1,844lb
  Cargo: 250lb

Loadings
  Pilot

Armament
  Two 30-mm MK 108 cannons.

Flight performance
  Maximum airspeed:
  560mph

Tow-planes: Bf 109G; Fw 190

Other Developments

As the Germans continued to use gliders on their many fronts, their experience provided them with a fund of data pointing to technical improvements which would give gliders greater operational effectiveness and pilots a greater margin of safety, and would create newer and better gliders. Some of the technical innovations got nowhere, excellent though they were. Others were developed, like the V-1 and V-2 powered glide-bombs, which were an outgrowth of the glider as the world well knows.

One of the early German experiments with gliders was known as the *Mistelschlepp*. It consisted of securing a fighter aeroplane to the top of a glider, so that the power of the fighter assisted the tow plane in lifting both into the air. The combination flew successfully many times. The Germans foresaw in this system a way of getting gliders to targets quickly; once released, the fighter would stand by overhead to provide protective cover. It also foresaw an explosive-laden glider as a missile, guided by radio to its target by the pilot of the fighter. Why this combination was not further exploited is not fully known. It is reported reliably that it had a long history, having been seen in flight over Czechoslovakia after the Germans seized that country but before World War II started. From this concept grew the idea of carrying a powered aeroplane into the air, its nose fused, and loaded to capacity with explosives; a powered missile to be released and guided by remote control to its target.

Rockets were also extensively used to give gliders their own propulsion, and thereby to help the tow-plane to get the glider into the air. Rocket-assisted take-offs were common practice with all models of gliders used in combat in the latter stages of the war. Rockets were also used for braking gliders when they made their landings. The Germans were the first to have a parachute brake, a deployable

Rigid-tow bar appended to the tail of a Junkers Ju 52 used primarily in DFS 230 rigid-tow flight

Close-up of coupling mechanism

Rigid-tow combination inflight

parachute at the end of the fuselage that the pilot could activate to allow him to bring his glider into a small or constricted landing area.

To give gliders greater manoeuvrability, and to extend their gliding range once released from tow-planes near their targets, the Argus impulse thruster was available, but it was never extensively used.

As a result of the problem that confronted the Luftwaffe of providing fighter escort for long-range bombers, there began in 1940 a series of experiments with aircraft tow combinations intended to increase the operational range of the fighters being fuelled by a glider in close tow. This was the starting point of a number of tests on towing possibilities, which led to the *Starrschlepp*, the non-flexible tow-bar. It consisted of a metal rod from one to ten meters in length with a ball and socket joint at both ends. It was wired internally or externally, between tug and glider, for intercommunication. The bar was releaseable by either the towing aircraft or the glider. By using this development the disadvantage of blind glider-flying was reduced, the strain of night flying was eased, and intercommunication was made superior to that of any other system of tow. The *Starrschlepp* failed to be more exploited because each Ju 52 aircraft used with it required modification for its installation. The rapidly changing war situation made the demand for these aircraft so great that time for making the alterations could not be afforded. Nonetheless, the *Starrschlepp* was extensively used for towing at night in the latter part of the war when Allied control of the airspace over Germany during daylight hours made it suicidal to use gliders in daylight missions.

The Luftwaffe learned through their intelligence of the system of glider pick-up used by the USAAF and conducted considerable research to develop such a system, but they were unsuccessful.

THREE

The British Glider Effort

When the British realised that the road to Dunkirk had begun with the crushing defeat of Fort Eben Emael in Belgium by a small German gliderborne force, they quickly took stock of their airborne doctrine and resources. Not surprisingly, their strategy was completely devoid of any reference to the use of airborne troops, and there was absolutely no aircraft designed for dropping paratroopers. The term 'transport glider' was unknown, so flagrant had been the British oversight before Dunkirk.

Sir Winston Churchill got the matter off dead centre in his characteristic way, by ordering the creation of a 5,000-man airborne force—P.M.W. (Prime Minister's Wishes), i.e. no questions asked. This order led to a glider construction programme started partly, because the British did not have enough powered aircraft to carry 5,000 paratroopers. Some of the lift had to come from another source, and obviously this source had to be the glider.

The amount of airborne lift Britain had mustered by some three years later was phenomenal. Glider production in Britain, until then practically nonexistent, was one of the extraordinary achievements of British industry, calling for prodigious efforts at all levels. In its glider production effort during World War II British industry showed itself at its best, and produced in quality and quantity, under great hardships and handicaps, what no other nation could hope to exceed.

Hadrian

The British Hadrian glider was actually the U.S. Air Force's Waco CG-4A, described in detail under the heading of U.S. gliders. (See pp. 103–13) While pilots of the British Glider Pilot Regiment, by and large, preferred to fly the Horsa, the Hadrian proved a valuable adjunct to British transport glider resources. From the British standpoint, the Hadrian was definitely considered to be primarily a troop transport glider. Trucks and artillery would be transported in the Horsa or the Hamilcar. The Royal Air Force procured 740 CG-4A's from the United States, and these were given the name Hadrian.

Hamilcar

The Hamilcar was the largest glider built by the Allies, a true monster of an aircraft, and a daring gamble. It prompted Colonel Frederick R. Dent, Chief of the U.S. Army Air Force's glider procurement pro-

General Aircraft Ltd Hamilcar, largest all-wood production glider to be used in operations in World War II

gramme, to remark while visiting British glider activities, 'It was the biggest hunk of airplane I have ever seen put together!'

In deciding to build the Hamilcar the British reasoned that should their strategy develop in such a way as to call for the commitment of large airborne forces, such a glider would be needed to transport tanks, large guns and vehicles, and huge amounts of ammunition and other stores, to give the airborne forces not only holding power, but a strong and aggressive punch.

General Aircraft Limited designed and built the Hamilcar at their Railway Carriage and Wagon Company plant at Birmingham. The design for the glider was finally agreed to early in 1941. Since it was considered advisable to design and construct a half-scale flying model, a team of a hundred draftsmen and twenty engineers and technicians jumped to the task, backed up by the facilities of the Royal Aircraft Establishment and the National Physical Laboratory, which handled the development of structural and wind-tunnel data. The model proved successful and General Aircraft soon built the full-scale glider.

The Hamilcar was the largest wooden aircraft built during World War II. To carry with structural and aerodynamic efficiency the weights it had to lift, it was necessary to select a wing loading much greater than anything previously contemplated for a glider. This wing loading came to 21.7lb per square foot.

It was a high-wing, cantilever monoplane with a wing span of 110 feet and a wing area of 1,657 square feet. The wing was of wood, with a centre section and two tapering outer sections. The inner structure had two box spars with laminated plywood booms and plywood webs, augmented with ribs. A thin plywood sheet covered the wing, and over this there was a fabric cover.

The fuselage, made of wood, was rectangular in shape, and constructed in two separate main sections which could be separated to facilitate its transport by ground to assembly points. The body was so constructed as to enable its plywood surface to carry a substantial part of the stresses developed, from whatever source. The bulbous nose was hinged on the starboard side and swung open for loading.

The decision to design the craft as a high-wing monoplane with a nose-opening door was made so as to ensure that with the aircraft lowered on to its skids, armoured track vehicles could be driven straight out without the need for special ramps. The vehicles could therefore be in action as little as fifteen seconds after the aircraft had come to rest. To speed its exit, the vehicle was started up while the glider was still in the air. The vehicle's exhaust pipes had temporary extensions to the outside of the glider; these disengaged as the vehicle moved forward. As the forward motion continued, a mechanical device freed the nose-door lock and automatically opened the door.

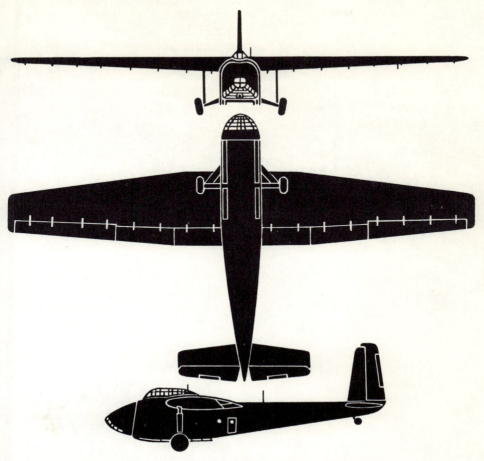

General Aircraft Hamilcar, three-view section

Although the craft was initially constructed with wheels which could be dropped, leaving it to land on skids, the technique was changed to keep the wheels for landing. This allowed pilots to taxi some distance to get clear of landing strips. When the glider came to rest, the high oil-pressure in the chassis shock-absorber struts was released, causing them to telescope, and permitting the glider to sink on to its skids so that the vehicle inside could drive out.

Two pilots, each with controls, sat in tandem in splendid isolation in the cockpit. A bullet-proof windshield protected them from the front and sides, while armour-plating protected them from the rear. They had telephone communication with the crews of vehicles below and the pilot of the towing aeroplane.

General Aircraft Hamilcar transporting light tank, exploded drawing

Loading a light tank into a General Aircraft Hamilcar

The Hamilcar could carry a Tetrarch Mark IV tank or a Locust tank, two Bren-gun universal carriers or two armoured scout cars, a 25-pound gun with tractor, or similar loads.

Because of its 'all-up' weight of 36,000 pounds, it needed an enormously powerful aircraft to tow it. During early tests a Halifax with souped-up engines was used. Later, as the Halifax bomber was modified to increase its engine power, a standard Halifax became the tug for the Hamilcar, although the Lancaster and Stirling four engined bombers were also used on occasion.

The first full-sized prototype flew on 27 March, 1942. During the course of the war 412 Hamilcars were built. They saw yeoman service in Normandy, at Wesel, and at Arnhem.

One Hamilcar was procured by the U.S. Army Air Forces for test and evaluation at its Air Force Materiel Command at Wright Army Air Force Field near Dayton, Ohio. Design studies were made to determine the feasibility of operating the Hamilcar in a 'pick-a-back' system, in conjunction with the U.S. P-38 fighter, (See U.S. Other Technical Developments, p. 157.)

A later British development was the Hamilcar X, which was a two-engined powered Hamilcar. It proved a very successful aeroplane.

Technical Data

Glider Model: Hamilcar
Type: heavy transport glider
Crew: pilot, co-pilot
Dimensions
  Wing-span: 110ft
  Wing area: 1,657sq ft
  Fuselage
    Length: 68.5ft
    Height: 20.3ft
  Cargo compartment
    Length: 25.5ft
    Width: 8ft
    Height: 7.5ft
Weight
  Total with cargo: 36,000lb
  Empty: 18,000lb
  Cargo: 17,500lb

Loadings
  One Tetrarch Mark IV tank, or 1 Locust tank, or 2 armoured scout cars, or 40 men, equipped or equivalent.
Flight performance
  Maximum towing speed: 150mph
  Maximum airspeed: 187mph
  Aspect ratio: 11.5
Tow-planes: Halifax, Lancaster, Stirling

Hengist

The Hengist was designed and built by Slingsby Sailplanes, Ltd. It was to carry fifteen troops, equipped. The Ministry of Aircraft Production placed the order at a time when the feasibility of constructing and producing in quantity anything as large as a 25-place glider was in doubt.

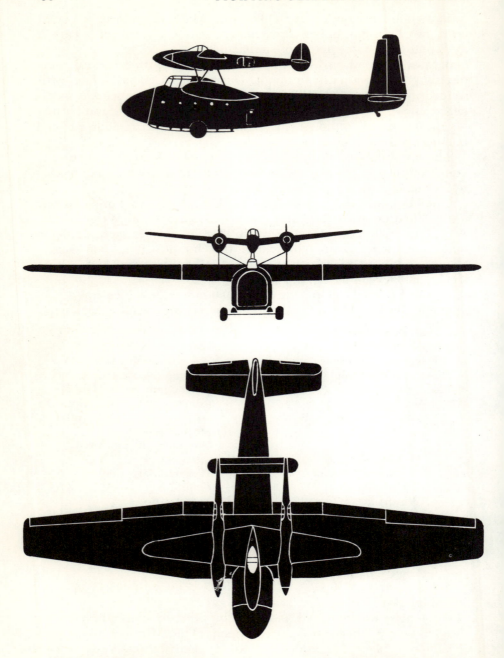

Concept of P-38, General Aircraft Hamilcar pick-a-back combination,
three-view section

Slingsby delivered the first model, in the latter part of 1942, to the Airborne Forces Experimental Establishment at Sherburn-in-Elmet in Yorkshire, near Leeds. As described by Lawrence Wright in *Wooden Wings*, it was '. . . a pretty aircraft, high-winged, slab-sided, obviously from the Slingsby stable'.

It incorporated some unique technical innovations. Made of wood throughout, except for some fittings, it had a wing-span of 80 feet, and a length of 56.6 feet. Wings had flaps along the trailing edges, and spoilers. The flaps were actuated by opening a scoop on the under surface of the wing. This drove air into the bellows within the flaps, forcing them to open downward. The flaps were raised while in flight by closing the scoop and opening a vent in the upper surface of the wing. This induced suction, which along with pressure of the air on the underside of the flaps, caused them to close. Lift spoilers were manually operated by lever from the cockpit which caused the spoilers to open out from the upper surfaces of the wings.

The undercarriage had brakes and could be jettisoned, after which the glider landed on a pneumatic skid running the length of the cabin, and also on a small pneumatic skid at the tail. No flight-test was conducted using the skids, however. The pilot and co-pilot had a full system of dual controls for flaps, spoilers and wheel brakes between their seats, as well as an elevator wheel, which was also between the seats.

Tests showed that in towed flight, control was good, though a slight stiffness in the ailerons was reported. The glider flew comfortably with the rudder free and with the pilot using only one hand. It also performed well in free flight, with no tendency to snatch, oscillate, or take charge. The flaps were very effective, but test pilots reported fluttering at all free flight speeds, and some tail heaviness when flaps had been activated.

Technical Data

Glider Model: Hengist
Type: transport glider
Crew: pilot, co-pilot
Dimensions
  Wing-span: 80ft
  Wing area: 780sq ft
  Fuselage
   Length: 56.6ft
Weight
  Total with cargo: 8,333lb
  Empty: 4,666lb
  Cargo: 3,667lb

Loadings
  Fifteen troops, equipped
Flight performance
  Maximum airspeed:
  160mph
  Stalling speed
   Flaps up: 45mph
   Flaps down: 40mph
  Aspect ratio: 8.21

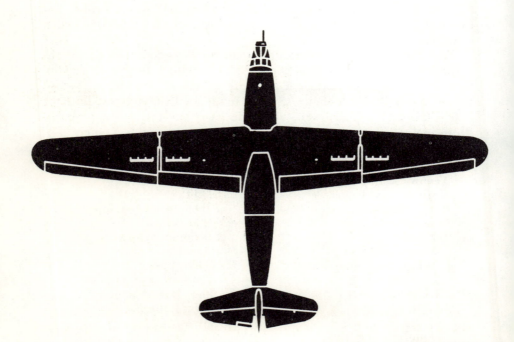

Slingsby Hengist, three-view section

Slingsby Hengist

Slingsby Hengist in flight

Slingsby built eighteen Hengists. One was soon to be written off, when a rigger omitted a wing-root pin, and the glider shed a wing near Dishforth. Fortunately the pilot, John Nielan survived, although after some months in the hospital.

Horsa (Mark I and II)

The Horsa, without a doubt, was the most ungainly-looking glider ever produced, and the ugly duckling of all World War II gliders. It prompted the remark that the inside of its long fuselage looked like a section of the London Underground Railway in miniature.

Intent on conserving critical metals as well as drawing upon wood-working industries not yet heavily involved in war-time production, the Air Ministry in specifications issued to the Airspeed Aviation Company, Ltd. in December 1940 called for the glider to be of wooden construction. So well did the design team (headed by Hessell Tiltman) comply, that H. A. Taylor, in *Airspeed Aircraft Since* 1931, was prompted to say it '. . . must have been the most wooden aircraft ever built. Even the controls in the cockpit were masterpieces of the woodworker's skill'.

According to Taylor, Tiltman carried out his design efforts at the de Havilland Technical School at Hatfield and later at Salisbury Hall, London Colney, after he had been bombed out of the technical schools. Airspeed assembled the first two prototypes at the Great West Road aerodrome, now part of Heathrow Airport. Five more were built at Airspeed's Portsmouth works, and they went on to build 700 production models there. By 10 September 1941, only nine months after the specification was issued, G. B. S. Errington test-flew the first Horsa at the Great West Road aerodrome.

Airspeed built two Horsa models, the Mark I and the Mark II. They were similar in external appearance. The Horsa was a high-wing monoplane with a large plexiglass nose and a jettisonable tricycle landing gear. The Mark I had a wing span of 88 feet and fuselage length of 67 feet. To the top of the fin it stood 19.5 feet high. The fuselage was circular in cross section, its plywood skin attached to stout circular wooden ribs. Light wooden benches ran down each side, with a three-seat bench across the rear.

The Mark I was originally conceived as a paratrooper transport, to drop paratroopers over target while under tow, and then be towed back to friendly territory to land. For the use of paratroopers. it had two passenger doors, one on either side of the fuselage, which were widely separated for simultaneous exits and which were designed to be slid upward to enable paratroopers to jump out or fire guns at attacking aircraft. Other firing points were an aperture in the roof aft of the main spar and a trap door in the tail. The firing points, however, were never used in action. The parachutist's static line would be attached to a short rail just over each parachute-door; the parachutist would hook his line to this rail on approaching the door just before making his exit. Supporting arms and supplies were to be dropped in containers and panniers.

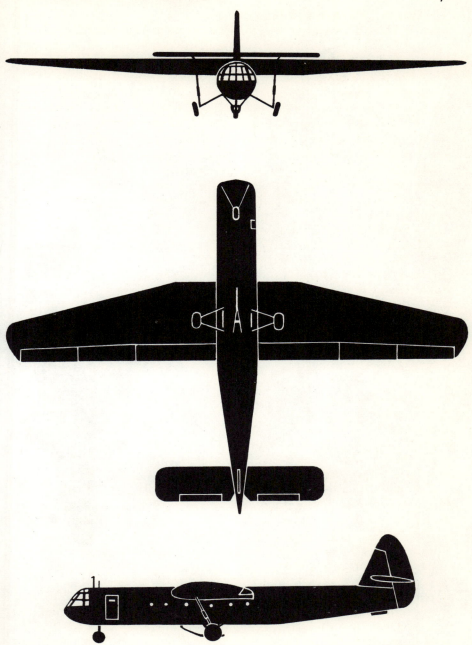

Airspeed Horsa, three-view section

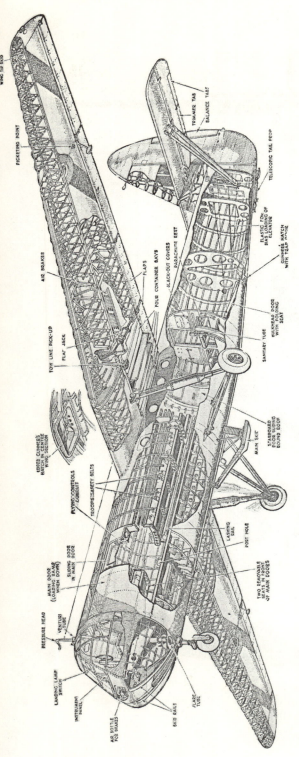

Airspeed Horsa and (*above*) exploded drawing

WING TIP SKID

PICKETING POINT

TRIMMER TAB

BALANCE TABS

TELESCOPIC TAIL PROP

ELASTIC FOR
BIAS LOADING OF
ELEVATOR

GUNNERS HATCH
WITH TRAP DOOR

AIR BRAKES

FLAPS

FOUR CONTAINER BAYS

BLACK-OUT COVERS

PARACHUTE REST

TOW LINE PICK-UP

FLAP JACK

SANITARY TUBE

BULKHEAD DOOR
WITH FOLDING
SEAT

UPPER GUNNERS
HATCH IN CENTRE
WING SECTION

FLYING CONTROLS
CONDUIT

TROOPS SAFETY BELTS

MAIN SKID

STARBOARD
DOOR SLIDING
ROUND ROOF

LASHING RAIL

POST HOLE

TWO REMOVABLE
SEATS IN FRONT
OF MAIN DOORS

PRESSURE HEAD

VENTURI TUBE

MAIN DOOR
(LOADING RAMP
WHEN DOWN)

SLIDING DOOR
IN MAIN DOOR

LANDING LAMP
SWITCH

INSTRUMENT
PANEL

AIR BOTTLE
FOR BRAKES

SKID RAILS

FLARE TUBE

The Mark I also had a rectangular loading door in the port side just aft of the nose. This measured 7.8 feet by 5 feet and was hinged at the bottom edge so that it could be lowered and used as an unloading ramp. The ramp was rarely used for loading because of its rather steep angle to the interior of the glider, and also because in loading it might be damaged and thus ground the glider. For loading vehicles troops could use troughs (ramps), each 11.8 feet long, in lieu of the door.

Originally the only vehicles carried with the glidermen were motor-cycles, although jeeps could be loaded with difficulty. With the necessity of manoeuvring heavy equipment such as a jeep around the corner of the cargo door, loading time proved excessively long and means were sought to reduce it. Airspeed carried out experiments in early 1944 to remove the tail by means of a band of cordex explosive placed along the rib at the end of the cargo compartment. On land-ing, a designated soldier blew off the rear of the Horsa; the troughs were then placed from the floor of the rear of the compartment to the ground and vehicles were driven out of the rear of the glider. Al-though a drastic solution, it worked successfully, and this 'surcingle', as it was termed, was used in the Normandy landings. Meanwhile the R.A.F. devised a means of making the tail a separate unit, bolted to the main fuselage by eight bolts with ingenious quick-release nuts. As standard equipment, Horsas carried powerful wire cutters. When the tail came off to unload equipment in combat, one of the pilots, or an airborne trooper, had the responsibility of cutting the glider control cables, leading to the empennage control surfaces, with the wire cut-ters. Airspeed modified many Horsas before the Normandy invasion with the quick-release nut system, but the surcingles were still carried in those gliders for emergency use. The Mark I's without the later modification were termed 'white' Horsas, those with it were 'red'.

The Mark II Horsa was designed to resolve the inconvenient problems of loading and unloading heavy equipment inherent in the Mark I. It had a hinged nose that could be swung open to enable the loading of jeeps and other heavy equipment. It was realised that the nose of a glider is particularly vulnerable, in a combat landing, to damage which might jam the nose door and prevent it from opening, or otherwise prevent unloading from the front of the cargo compart-ment; so the rear unloading system of the 'red' Horsas was built into the Mark II's, which became known as 'blue' Horsas.

The Mark II carried 28 fully-armed troops, a pilot and a co-pilot. In lieu of an equivalent weight of men, it could transport two Jeeps ($\frac{1}{4}$-ton trucks), a 75-mm howitzer and a $\frac{1}{4}$-ton truck, or an assortment of other gear or ammunition weighing up to 7,380lb. The Mark I carried 250 pounds less.

Components of an Airspeed Horsa

The Mark II was towed using a 'Y' tow-rope with the top ends of the Y hitched one on each side of the forward edge of the wing; the rope for the Mark I hitched just forward of the nose wheel. The normal flying position of the Horsa was immediately behind and slightly higher than the tug-plane.

In early models a telephone system provided a means for the tug-pilot and the glider-pilot to talk to each other. Telephone conversation terminated when the glider cut away from the aeroplane, to the disadvantage of the glider pilot. Later in the war the R.A.F. had radios placed in all Horsas, enabling aeroplane pilots and glider pilots to communicate with each other even after the glider had landed.

Despite its ponderous appearance the Horsa performed well. It towed at a maximum speed of 160 miles per hour. Extra large 'barn-door' flaps permitted a steep angle of descent. At the same time they throttled the speed build-up during glider descent. The Horsa landed on concrete runways or ploughed fields with almost equal ease. When pilots used the enormous flaps and the pneumatic wheel-brakes, the ungainly craft could be brought successfully into surprisingly small fields.

In addition to the Mark I and II, Airspeed built a Horsa bomber and a powered Horsa for experimental purposes. The former had a bomb bay built to carry either 2,000, 4,000 or 8,000lb bombs. The powered glider was fitted with two 375hp Armstrong-Siddeley Cheetah X radial engines. A much larger model of the Horsa was also

Technical Data

Glider Model: Horsa Mark II
Type: transport glider, also for paratroop drops
Crew: pilot, co-pilot
Dimensions
  Wing-span: 88ft
  Wing area: 1,104sq ft
  Fuselage
   Length: 68ft
   Height: 20.3ft
  Cargo compartment
   Length: 34ft
   Width: 7.5ft
   Height: 10.5ft
Weight
  Total with cargo: 15,750lb
  Empty: 8,370lb
  Cargo: 7,380lb

Loadings
Two $\frac{1}{4}$-ton 4 × 4 trucks; or 28 troops, equipped; or one USA M3A1 75 mm howitzer plus one $\frac{1}{4}$-ton 4 × 4 truck plus ammunition and crew.

Flight performance
Towing speed: 160mph
Maximum airspeed with flaps: 100mph
Stalling speed
  Flaps up: 58mph
  Flaps down: 48mph
Aspect ratio: 7.2

Tow-planes: Albemarle, Halifax, C-47

Loading an Airspeed Horsa

Some General Aircraft Horsas had cordite explosive between the tail and main fuselage sections. After landing (and after passengers were clear of the glider) the cordite was exploded to sever the sections and enable the rapid unloading of equipment through the opening created. This photo was taken after D-Day landings

built, but remained in the experimental class with the bomber and powered versions.

Horsas carried British and American airborne troops into Norway, Sicily, Normandy, Arnhem, Yugoslavia and across the Rhine at Wesel. They also served in Palestine, and numbers of them were shipped to India and Canada.

Hotspur (Mark I, II and III)

The Hotspur was the first transport glider produced by the Allies. It was a graceful craft that, from a design standpoint, was the stepping stone from the frail, swallow-like sailplane to the enormous transport gliders that were soon to be on the drawing boards. As a matter of fact, it retained enough of the characteristics of the sailplane to indicate that the aircraft industry had not yet grasped the concept of what form a transport glider should take or just how to attain the objective of carrying tons of equipment on glider wing.

The original conception was of an 8-seater glider with a very long landing approach and a glide angle not steeper than 1 in 24. The craft was to be used for one flight only—to be completely expendable, in other words.

The General Aircraft Company Ltd. got the requirements for the glider in June 1940. Surprisingly, General was able to produce the first aircraft in little over four months, and the first flight took place on 5 November 1940.

The Hotspur Mark I had a wing-span of 62 feet. The top of the fuselage could be detached and cast off by the troops inside, to allow them to jump over the sides of the boat-shaped bottom half.

The Mark II was a pronounced departure in design from the Mark I. This change came for two reasons. First, it was determined that the glider should be used to drop paratroopers. Secondly, towcraft were to take the glider right into the landing zone at low altitude, so the glider would need a steep, fast approach to land.

Thus the Mark II had a reduced wing-span measuring 46 feet, 16 feet shorter than the Mark I. This raised strength factors by fifty per cent and permitted a twenty per cent increase in the gliding angle. Doors were introduced to enable paratroopers to jump from the glider.

A third Hotspur, the Mark III, was designed for training. The main difference between the Mark II and III was that the former was towed from the keel and had an unbraced tailplane, whereas the latter was towed from the nose and had a braced tailplane.

The Hotspur models were mid-wing cantilever monoplanes. They had an oval fuselage of wooden structure with a stressed plywood skin. Pilots sat in tandem, each at his controls. There were two cabins, one

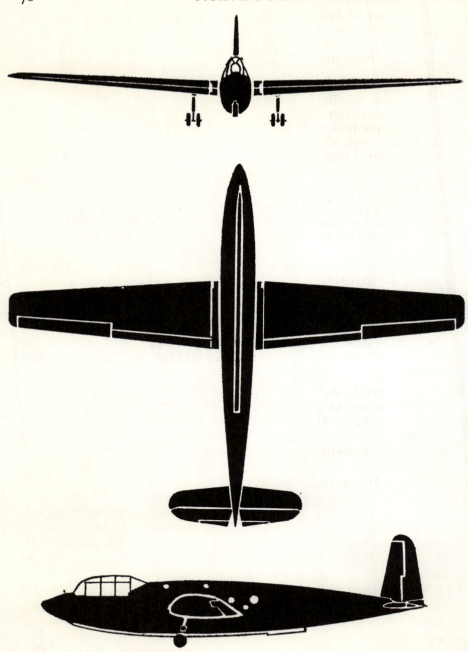

General Aircraft Hotspur II, three-view section

General Aircraft Hotspur about to land

Troops loading into a General Aircraft Hotspur

Interior of a General Aircraft
Hotspur

Interior of a General Aircraft
Hotspur looking aft

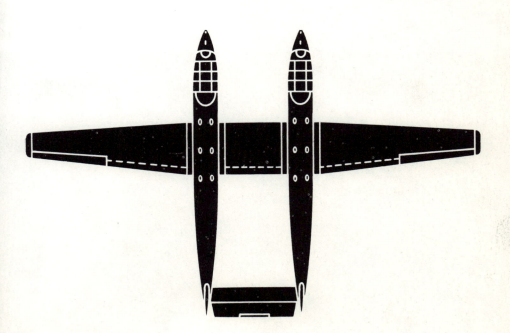

General Aircraft twin Hotspur, three-view section

fore and one aft of the wing structure, each with its own access door. Access to the pilot's compartment was by a hinged canopy. The wheels could be jettisoned.

Eighteen Mark I's were built, and 997 Mark II's. Fifty Mark II's were converted into Mark III's. Although extensively used for training by the Glider Pilot Regiment, Hotspurs were never used in combat.

Technical Data

Glider Model: Hotspur,
    Mark II
Type: transport glider
Crew: pilot
Dimensions
    Wing-span: 45.9ft
    Wing area: 272sq ft
    Fuselage
      Length: 39.7ft
      Height: 10.8ft

Weight
    Total with cargo: 3,635lb
    Empty: 1,755lb
    Cargo: 1,880lb
Loadings
    Seven troops, equipped.
Tow-planes: Hawker Hector
    or Audaxe

General Aircraft twin Hotspur

Twin Hotspur

This glider was conceived as a method of lifting greater loads, using components of the Hotspur. It consisted of two Hotspur fuselages, secured to each other by a special centre section. It was an innovative design, and more than doubled the effective cargo capacity of the Hotspur. It could carry the pilot, co-pilot and fourteen glidermen, a total of sixteen persons, eight in each fuselage. The pilots were in the port fuselage, from which they controlled the glider.

The Twin had a wing-span of 58 feet, a length of 39.7 feet, and was 10.5 feet high. The wing area was 262 square feet. It weighed 3,025 pounds empty and carried 3,525 pounds. It was towed at 150mph.

This glider was soon discarded, since, although it transported considerably more than the Hotspur, it had some of the Hotspur's disadvantages; the difficulty of getting out when the glider landed, and less than desirable cargo capacity. Although in the Twin the cargo capacity had been increased, motorcycles and light trucks, while within the weight capacity of the glider, could still not be loaded because of the design of the glider.

Only one was built.

FOUR

Japanese Transport Gliders

In 1937, during the Sino-Japanese War, the Japanese ordered three test gliders built, the Tachikawa Ki-23 and -25, and the Fukada Ki-24. The Ki-23 was a single-place glider, the others were 2-place models. The Fukada proved an excellent glider and was produced as the Hikara-6-I, in a civilian version.

When World War II started, news filtered through to Japan that transport gliders had been used by the Germans in their invasion of the West. Based on this information, and their experience with the Ki-series gliders, the Army launched a transport glider programme. Work on the first glider began in June 1940, one month after the German glider assault on Fort Eben Emael in Belgium.

The Army designated its series Ku from the word *kakku*, to glide. The Japanese Navy, in a parallel action, launched a glider development programme of its own.

Ku-1

The first Japanese glider to be built was the Ku-1. Professor Hiroshi Sato, of the Imperial University's engineering school of Kyushu, designed the glider, and the Maeda Aircraft Corporation manufactured it.

The first model was a shoulder-wing, twin-boom, twin-fin glider with a wing-span of over 55 feet. The Corporation completed it in the summer of 1941 and tested it at the Tachiarai military airfield in Kyushu on 1 September 1941.

Technical Data

Glider Model: Ku-I, -II, -III
Type: transport glider
Crew: pilot, co-pilot
Dimensions
  Wing-span: 55ft
  Wing area: 324sq ft
  Fuselage
    Length: 32ft
Weight
  Total with cargo: 2,860lb
  Empty: 1,540lb
  Cargo: 1,320lb

Loadings
  Eight troops, equipped.
Flight performance
  Maximum towing speed: 80mph
  Maximum airspeed: 110mph
  Aspect ratio: 9.7
Tow-planes: Mitsubishi Ki-51 (Sonia), Ki-30

The Army soon accepted it, and produced it as a type 2 transport glider, Ku-1. It carried six to eight equipped troops and a pilot.

The Ku-1 was succeeded in the series by the Ku-2, the major modification being that the new glider had a transparent nose, a single boom and a longer fuselage. It did not go into production.

The final development in the series was the Ku-3, a model whose fuselage resembled a wing cross-section. The wing was tapered and had spoilers. It had accommodation for eight men in the absence of other cargo. It also did not go into production.

As larger gliders were produced, the Ku-1 was relegated to training use. Approximately 100 were produced.

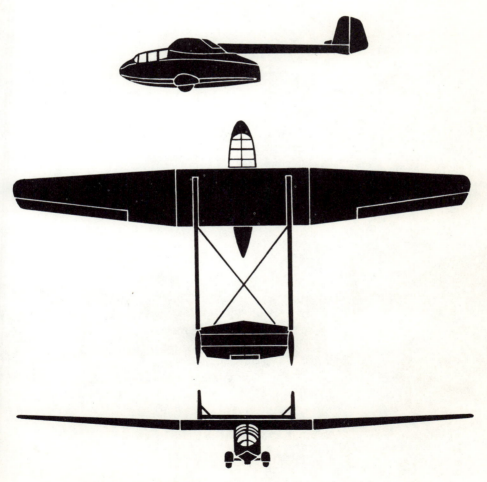

Maeda Ku-1-I, first Japanese transport glider, three-view section

Maeda Ku-1-I

Ku-1-I

Ku-6

After the Ku-1 series the Maeda Aircraft Corporation produced the Ku-6, one of the most interesting concepts in aircraft created by any nation during World War II. The Aeronautical Institute of the Imperial University in Tokyo did the actual design for Maeda. They designed it to the requirements set forth by the Army's Troop Transport Command.

The Army needed a quick means to move tanks long distances over the main islands of Japan to resist seaborne invasion. It conceived the idea that this could be done by equipping the tank with wings, empennage, and take-off carriage; once landed, the equippage to make the tank airborne could be rapidly detached to allow the tank to go into action as a ground vehicle. This is a concept not unlike that ordered by General 'Hap' Arnold of the U.S. Air Force. (See U.S. CG4A, pp. 103–13)

By late 1939 the Japanese Army Air Force Examination Department initiated Special Tank Project Number 3 that took the code name 'Sora-sha' (air vehicle). This later became 'Kuro-sha' (black vehicle). The Aeronautical Institute of the Imperial University in Tokyo designed the glider while Maedo Koken Kogyo (Maeda Air Research Industry) constructed the wing and empennage and Mitsubishi built the special tank and major structural components of the fuselage. The Sora-sha became the Ku-6, its glider series number.

The total weight of the Ku-6 was 7,712lb, of which 6,174lb was attributable to the weight of the light tank. Maeda completed the prototype in January 1945.

Technical Data

Glider Model: Ku-6
Type: 'winged' air-transportable tank
Crew: pilot, co-pilot
Dimensions:
  Wing-span: 72ft
  Wing area: 649sq ft

Weight
  Total with cargo: 7,712lb
  Empty: 1,538lb
  Cargo: 6,174lb
Loadings
  1 tank

Ku-7

The Ku-7, code-name 'Buzzard', also more popularly known as the *Manazuru* (flying crane), was the Japanese Army's most noteworthy large-sized transport glider. It filled the need for greater tactical and strategical mobility and striking power for army units, by enabling the quick movement of tanks and large numbers of troops. Although the doctrinal reasons for launching into the design and construction of this large glider were sound, it never went into mass production as a glider, and there is no record of its having been used in any operation.

The Kyoto branch of the Kokusai Aircraft Company built the glider and the Aviation Research Laboratory of Tokyo University assisted in designing the wing. The wing was tapered and was highly efficient aerodynamically. The design was based on the Japanese 'B' series wing section, and was patterned after the very successful Ki-77 Long Range Aircraft.

The glider had twin booms, each surmounted by vertical fins and connected by an elevator assembly. The fuselage pointed upward at the rear. In appearance it was very similar to the German Go 242

Manazuru Ku-7, three view section

glider. It had a tricycle landing gear, consisting of a nose wheel and two main wheels on each side placed in tandem.

Undertaken as a project in late 1942, the glider was first tested in August 1944. Standard towing aeroplanes for this large craft were the Nakajima Ki-49-II (HELEN) or the Mitsubishi Ki-67-I (PEGGY). Loading was carried out via the rear of the cargo compartment which had a swinging door made of the rear of the fuselage.

Nine Ku-7's were built; testing was not entirely completed when the war ended. So promising were the glider models, however, that it was decided to produce a powered version of the glider; this became known as the Ki-105 aeroplane. Forty Ki-105's were built, and became known as the *Ohtori*.

Technical Data

Glider Model: Ku-7
Type: heavy transport glider
Crew: pilot, co-pilot
Dimensions
  Wing-span: 114ft
  Wing area: 1,288sq ft
  Fuselage
   Length: 64ft
  Cargo compartment
   Length: 17ft
   Width: 10ft
   Height: 7ft
Weight
  Total with cargo: 26,455lb
  Empty: 10,000lb
  Cargo: 16,455lb

Loadings
  8-ton tank, 32 troops, equipped, or a 7.5 mm cannon plus 4-ton tractor.
Flight performance
  Maximum towing speed: 125mph
  Maximum airspeed: 220mph
  Aspect ratio: 10.8
Tow-planes: Nakajima Ki 49-II; Mitsubishi Ki 67-I

Ku-8

In December 1941 a Ki-59 (THERESA) transport aeroplane was modified to transform it into a glider. The modifications were not extensive. They consisted primarily in removing the two engines, converting the undercarriage into one that could be dropped, and adding skids to the bottom of the fuselage. The new aircraft became the Ku-8-I experimental glider. It carried eighteen equipped troops. Later this model was drastically modified to effect an almost complete redesign of the original. The wing shape was changed as well as the fuselage.

In April 1943 this new version entered production as the large-sized transport glider, the Ku-8-II, or Gander. It was built at the Hiratsuka plant of the Kokusai Koku Aircraft Company, and accepted after a round trip flight between Fussa and Okinawa in August.

Manazuru Ku-7. Note the similarities to the German Gotha Go 242

Twin engined KI-105 (powered Manazuru Ku-7 glider)

Kokusai Ku-8-II, three-view section

The wing was 76 feet long and constructed with two main spars. Plywood covered the wing forward of the lead spar, and the whole wing was covered with fabric. One of the most unconventional features of this glider and one that makes it unique among all aircraft is that its spoilers were separate; four-foot-long wings set a foot above the main wing on either side of the fuselage and along the wings' trailing edge. To reduce lift, the spoilers could be rotated as much as ninety degrees from the horizontal. The fuselage was of welded tubular steel. The nose was of plexiglass and had no framework structure that would obstruct the pilot's ability to see the tow-rope and tow-plane.

Kokusai Ku-8-II and (*below*) with spoilers

Kokusai Ku-8-II with ramps in position preparatory to loading a vehicle
or artillery piece

Nihon Kogata Ku-11

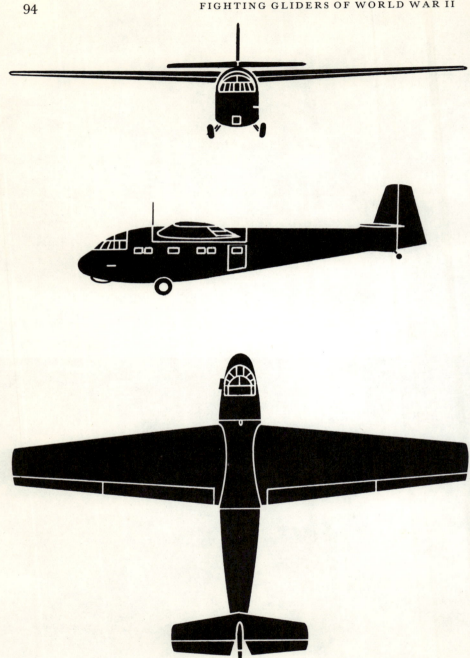

Nihon Kogata Ku-11, three-view section

The glider had dual controls, and a unique arrangement whereby the pilot had a wheel control, the co-pilot a stick. The length of the glider was 45 feet. It had landing wheels that could be dropped, enabling the glider to land on skids. Tie-down devices were part of the floor structure; vehicles and other gear could be lashed to these devices to prevent them from shifting in flight. The nose of the fuselage opened sideways to permit cargo to be loaded.

The Ku-8-II was towed by a Mitsubishi Ki-21 (SALLY) heavy bomber. In tests, wings began to flutter at speeds greater than 225 miles per hour; pilots took the view that the glider was a clumsy aircraft, difficult to handle.

However, one reliable report indicates the Japanese Army had 700 Ku-8's built. A number of Ku-8's were found by American forces at Nichols Field near Manila on the island of Luzon in the Philippines after the Japanese surrendered.

Technical Data

Glider Model: Ku-8-II
Type: Transport glider
Crew: pilot, co-pilot
Dimensions
   Wing-span: 76ft
   Wing area: 544sq ft
   Fuselage
   Length: 45ft
   Cargo compartment
   Length: 10ft
   Width: 6.3ft
   Height: 5.6ft

Weight
   Total with cargo: 7,700lb
   Empty: 3,750lb
   Cargo: 3,950lb
Loadings
   Eighteen troops, equipped, miscellaneous cargo, or one small mountain artillery piece.
Flight performance
   Maximum airspeed: 150mph
   Towing speed: 120mph

Tow-planes: Mitsubishi-21-II, Ki-57-II, Ki-67-I

Ku-11

There is very little information available about the Ku-11. The Nihon Small Plane Manufacturing Company produced it as an experimental glider, and it became known as the Nihon Kogata Army Experimental Transport Glider Ku-11. Mr. Miyahara designed it.

Technical Data

Glider Model: Ku-11
Type: Transport glider
Crew: pilot, co-pilot
Dimensions
   Wing-span: 60ft
   Wing area: 475sq ft

Weight
   Total with cargo: 5,400lb
   Empty: 2,800lb
   Cargo: 2,600lb

It was a high-wing transport glider intended for landing troops at strategic locations to counter enemy invasion efforts. It carried twelve fully equipped troops.

The Ku-11 was to have been built in small subcontracting wood-working shops. It never went into production because the army was indecisive about its use and suspended further developments.

MXY5, MXY5a

During August 1941 the Japanese Navy ordered its Experimental Aeronautics Board to produce a towed glider transport for airborne forces. The specifications required that it should carry a pilot and co-pilot and eleven troops, that it should be towable by either a Mitsu-bishi G3M (Nell) or a G4M (Betty) bomber, and that it should be capable of becoming airborne under tow in a distance of 2,700 feet. Another specification was that either of the tow craft should be able to tow two gliders.

The Japan Aircraft Corporation built the MXY5, with Mr Yama-moto, a civil engineer, as its chief designer. The glider incorporated the most advanced ideas in aircraft design, and employed the latest techniques in manufacturing and metallurgy.

The result was an exceptionally fine aircraft. The wing was a high cantilever, a tapered design 59.4 feet long. The main wing spar was of duraluminium. The wings had flaps and spoilers. The ribs were of wood, and the whole wing was covered with plywood, with cloth over the plywood. The fuselage had a tubular steel framework and was also covered with plywood and fabric.

There were dual controls, droppable landing wheels, and a single skid running from the nose to midpoint on the bottom of the fuselage. The wheels were retractable and were retracted when the glider was used for training. They could be dropped after take-off when the glider was on an operational mission.

The glider was tested in 1942 at the Kasumiga-Ura Air Base, a naval training centre north-east of Tokyo, and passed all tests success-fully. Between 1942 and July 1945 the Navy had nine MXY5's and three MXY5a's built. The glider was never used operationally.

Technical Data

Glider Model: MXY5, 5A
Type: transport glider
Crew: pilot, co-pilot
Dimensions
  Wing-span: 59.4ft
  Wing area: 475sq ft
  Fuselage
    Length: 43ft

Weight
  Total with cargo: 5,940lb
  Empty: 3,530lb
  Cargo: 2,240lb
Loadings
  2,240 pounds of cargo, or
  11 troops, equipped.
Tow-planes: Mitsubishi G3M
  or AG4M

FIVE

The United States Glider Programme

In February 1941 the U.S. Army Air Corps found that 'In view of certain information received from abroad. . .' a study should be initiated on developing a glider that could be towed by aircraft. General Henry H. 'Hap' Arnold, Chief of the Army Air Corps, directed the initiation of this study on 25 February, and requested that by 1 April 1941 his staff should prepare a statement recommending the desirable characteristics of a military transport glider.

Arnold was the first American military leader to demonstrate interest in the possible worth of a transport glider as a military weapon. Shortly thereafter the United States set a breathtaking pace in glider development and procurement, involving countless companies in design and construction. Specialised aircraft companies, furniture factories, piano companies, a casket maker and even a pickle company entered into the massive effort.

Almost 16,000 transport and training gliders were produced for the military services. 13,909 of these were CG-4A's; there were more CG-4a's manufactured during the war than any other single model of aeroplane except for the B-24 heavy bomber, the P-47 and the P-51.

The procurement of all gliders involved twenty-three companies in ten states in the development of experimental models; it involved twenty-two companies in fourteen states in eleven production models. In the effort, almost 500 million dollars was expended, a considerable amount for the 1940s.

The AAF shipped 5,991 CG-4A's, 87 CG-15A's and 81 CG-13A's to the European theatre of operations. It sent 2,303 CG-4A's to the Mediterranean and six to China-Burma-India from the United States, additional numbers later being shipped there from other theatres. Air Force units in the South Pacific received 504 CG-4A's and five YCG-13A's and Great Britain 740 CG-4A's and six CG-13A's, making a grand total of 9,723 U.S. gliders shipped overseas.

Shortly after the programme began, the Army Air Corps (to be redesignated the Army Air Forces (AAF) on 20 June 1941 and assume the status of an independent service) set up a Glider Branch in the AAF's Materiel Command at Wright Field near Dayton, Ohio. This branch became the focal point for the development and procurement of transport gliders for the AAF. The Materiel Command carried out many research and testing projects at the Clinton County Army Air Field near Wilmington, Ohio. The AAF's counterpart for the development of Navy gliders was the Naval Aircraft Factory in Philadelphia, Pennsylvania.

The AAF applied its standard aircraft nomenclature to transport gliders. As an example, the combination XCG-3 stood for (X) experimental, (C) cargo, (G) glider and the (3) for the third new glider model in the series of glider aircraft being produced. (T) meant training, and (B) stood for bomb in the training and bomb gliders respectively. The (A) in CG-3A meant that this glider was no longer experimental and had been accepted for production. When the (A) was changed to (B), as will be found with the CG-4B (see section on the CG-4A, p. 111), the (B) indicated a major modification of the production glider. When a glider went from the experimental to the production stage and was approved except for minor tests, the (X) was replaced with a (Y), thus XCG-13, became YCG-13. By this production action the AAF enabled companies to manufacture urgently-needed gliders without awaiting the completion of trials.

Army Air Corps and Air Force Gliders

XCG-1, -2

The Army Air Corps launched a glider development programme in May 1941 by signing a contract with the Frankfort Sailplane Company, located in Joliet, Illinois that called for Frankfort to build the XCG-1, an 8-place glider, and the XCG-2, a 15-place glider. The company was to build static-test and flight-test models of each.

At that time Frankfort was achieving recognised success in the construction of the XTG-1 Frankfort Utility Glider for the glider-pilot training programme, which was just getting under way. Because the company was already committed to the XTG-1, progress on the design and construction of the XCG-1 and -2 moved slowly. In December 1941 the company finally brought a static-test model of the XCG-1 to the Army Air Force (AAF) Materiel Command at Wright Field, Troy, Ohio, for test and evaluation. The model failed structural tests, and the AAF cancelled the XCG-1 and -2 contract.

CG-3A

The AAF meanwhile negotiated for the construction of other experimental gliders with the Waco Aircraft Company of Troy, Ohio. A contract, approved in June 1941, provided that they would build one static-test and one flight-test model of an 8-place XCG-3 glider, and one static-test and two flight-test models of a 15-place glider.

The company moved rapidly into design and construction of the wind-tunnel model. By September Waco reported they had completed wind-tunnel tests. By 26 December 1941 they delivered a

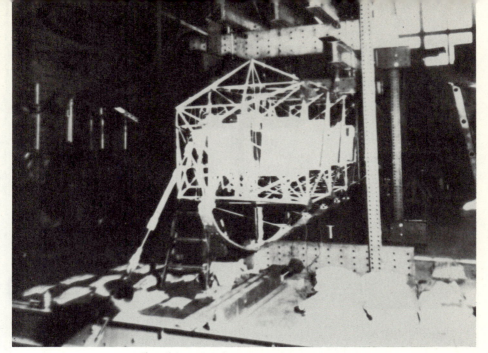

Frankfort XCG-1 under construction

Waco XCG-3

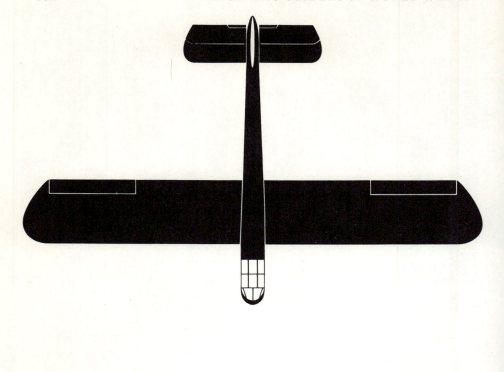

Waco CG-3A, three-view section

static-structural-test model and a flight-test model just one month later. Both models tested satisfactorily, and in April 1942 the AAF accepted the XCG-3 as satisfactory for quantity production.

The XCG-3 was a high-wing monoplane with strut braces, wooden wings and empennage construction. The fuselage was a frame of welded steel tubing covered with fabric. Like most early gliders it could be fitted with either of two landing gears: a semi-fixed one that was attached and used for training and a gear which could be detached by the pilot from the cockpit after the glider was airborne. The latter was available for combat operations and airborne manoeuvres. If the wheels were dropped, the glider landed on plywood skis attached to its underside.

The AAF made the decision to go into quantity production of an enlarged XCG-3 that would carry nine equipped troops, and designated it the CG-3A, Commonwealth Corporation of Kansas City, Missouri, being awarded the contract. But within a short time the AAF substantially reduced the procurement of the glider, turning instead to the more suitable XCG-4, which was well under way at Waco. Commonwealth built 100 CG-3A's before the contract's termination. The company then turned its technical know-how, gained from the CG-3A experience, to the building of the CG-4A.

The CG-3A's were shipped to many glider-pilot training bases in America, where the gliders were extensively flown in transition phases of training before the pilots began to fly the larger and heavier CG-4A.

Technical Data

Glider Model: CG-3A
Type: transport-training
  glider
Crew: pilot, co-pilot
Dimensions
  Wing-span: 73ft
  Wing area: 420sq ft
  Fuselage
    Length: 48.5ft

Weight
  Total with cargo: 4,400lb
  Empty: 2,400lb
  Cargo: 2,000lb
Loadings
  Seven troops, equipped
Flight performance
  Maximum towing speed:
  120mph

CG-4A

The CG-4A was probably the most awkward-looking glider produced by the U.S. during the war and at the same time one that handled best. One pilot, accustomed to the lines of graceful sailplanes, described the CG-4A as a 'ghastly sight!' Another remarked, 'It's all right to fly a box car, but why fly it sideways!'

On the credit side of the ledger, the CG-4A carried a large amount of cargo for its weight and could be flown safely by pilots lacking comprehensive training. This latter factor was a decided advantage

100 Waco CG-3As manufactured by the Commonwealth, parked at Kansas City airport awaiting shipment to glider pilot training centres in the U.S.

Waco CG-4A (Commonwealth forces Hadrian) glider workhorse of the American glider-force world-wide

in the early phases of planning glider operations, when the need for more than 30,000 trained glider pilots was projected.

Waco delivered the static-test model on 28 April 1942, and on 14 May the flight-test model. So urgent was the need for an acceptable transport glider that both were submitted to an accelerated test schedule. In a significant test a plane towed the XCG-4 from Wright Field to Chanute Field, Illinois, a distance of 220 miles.

Except for a minor change needed in the rudder and fin, the XCG-4 passed the test phase successfully, and it was declared acceptable on

Waco CG-4A, three-view section

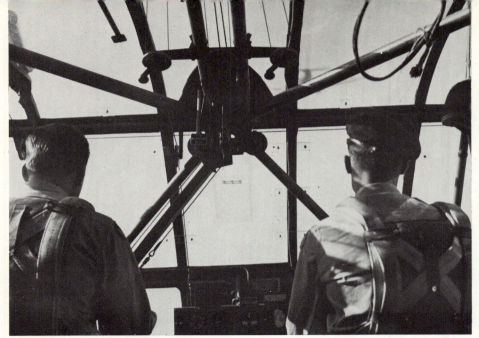

Cockpit of the Waco CG-4A. Note tow rope release lever (centre, left)

Waco CG-4As under construction

June 20, 1942. In this aircraft the Air Force found the solution to the urgent need for a reliable, easily manufactured combat glider.

In effect, the CG-4A was an enlarged version of the CG-3. General Harold H. 'Hap' Arnold, wrote in a directive: 'I would like very much to have a small light jeep constructed. . . to carry two men and have light armor and guns. This jeep should be designed and constructed with a view to fitting wings to it so that we can take off as a glider and drop it as a glider. Having dropped as a glider, it lands on a field somewhere, sheds its wings and goes around as a jeep.' Consequently the designers made the fuselage of the CG-4A commodious enough to carry the army's ¼-ton truck. To permit the truck to enter the glider, they conceived an unique design whereby the entire nose, containing the pilots' seats and controls, was hinged at the top of the fuselage. The nose could be elevated (swung) upward, thereby creating an opening into which the truck could be driven. To carry troops, box-like plywood three-man passenger seats were added, two on each side of the cargo area.

As other experimental gliders showed little promise of supplying an acceptable 15-place glider, the AAF entered into mass production of the CG-4A. Eleven companies were awarded contracts for a total of 640 of these gliders.

The CG-4A was a strut-braced, high-wing monoplane, which could carry more than its own empty weight. The wings, two spars and ribs were made of wood, the surface a thin sheet of plywood covered with fabric. The elevators were fabric-covered only. The wings had elliptical tips and little or no dihedral.

The fuselage was a welded steel tube frame covered with fabric. The floor was honeycomb plywood, a fabricating technique that gave strength and rigidity with little weight. The plywood structure was reinforced under the margins of the floor that bore the load of the ¼-ton truck wheels. As simply constructed as it appeared, nonetheless it had over 70,000 parts. Before the last CG-4A came off the production line its original design had been altered more than 7,000 times.

Waco designed a unique system to allow the jeep to go into action quickly, using the vehicle to raise the nose of the glider. After the jeep had been loaded into the glider, a cable was hitched to the pintle of the jeep. When the glider had landed and come to a halt, or even while yet airborne, the driver of the jeep started its motor. Glidermen cut or untied lashings holding the vehicle in place. The glider pilots hastily got out of the nose. The driver then drove slowly forward. As he did this, the cable pulled the nose up. The vehicle's wheels pushed the ramps, causing them to fall forward to the ground so the vehicle could drive out of the glider. When the nose had been raised fully it automatically locked, and when the jeep had driven a few more feet,

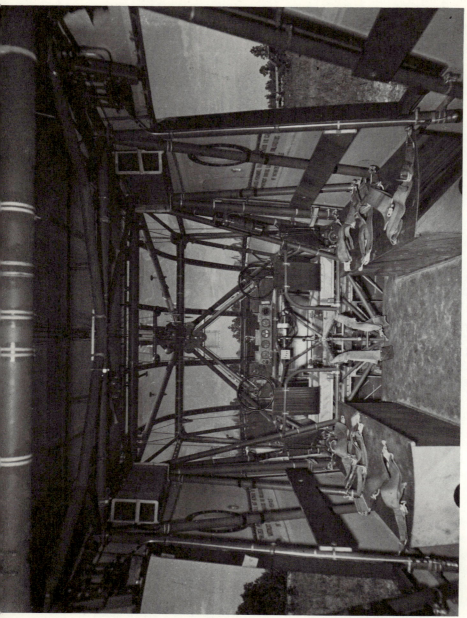

Interior of a Waco CG-4A

Waco CG-4A, brake parachute released, coming in for a landing

Waco CG-4A glider with Ludington-Griswold nose modification to give pilots added protection. Of the Wacos that flew in the Holland invasion, 700 had this modification, which saved many lives particularly in those fields in which the Germans had erected anti-glider posts (Rommel's asparagus)

Waco CG-4A in rigid tow behind a Douglas C-47

Waco CG-4A drops take-off wheels. It will land on skids. Early CG-4As landed on skids only. Later all CG-4As used wheels for landing gear

the cable automatically unhitched from the pintle of the jeep. The total procedure took but a few seconds to accomplish.

Early models of the CG-4A took off on wheels which were jettisoned above the take-off field, to be recovered later. They landed on plywood skids.

The CG-4A had dual wheel controls, placed side by side. It could be trimmed in respect to all three axes with three separate trim tab controls located above and between the pilots' seats. Instruments included the air-speed indicator, a 'sensitive' altimeter, a bank and turn indicator, and a rate of climb indicator. These were typical aircraft instruments of that period. They were manufactured for use in aircraft where engine vibrations kept gauges from sticking. Since they were not sensitive enough for the vibrationless gliders, wary pilots had to tap them from time to time to be certain they were registering accurately.

Later models had a two-way radio to enable the pilot to talk to his tow-pilot. Until then, glider and plane were connected by telephone. This was unsatisfactory, for the telephone wire, which was wrapped around the tow rope, was often bruised unavoidably or severed.

On 13 May 1942 the Material Command at Wright Field signed a contract with the Timm Aircraft Company of Los Angeles for the construction of a plywood fuselage for one CG-4A glider, thus insuring a satisfactory all-wood design for the CG-4 fuselage in the event of a shortage of steel tubing. In April 1943 Timm delivered the XCG-4B containing a wooden fuselage. In external appearance the glider was

Technical Data

Glider Model: CG-4A
Type: transport glider
Crew: pilot, co-pilot
Dimensions
  Wing-span: 83.6ft
  Wing area: 852sq ft
  Fuselage
    Length: 48ft
    Height: 7.3ft
  Cargo compartment
    Length: 13.2ft
    Width: 5.8ft
    Height: 7.2ft
Weight
  Total with cargo: 7,500lb
  Empty: 3,440lb
  Cargo: 4,060lb

Loadings
  One $\frac{1}{4}$-ton 4×4 truck with radio, driver, radio operator and one other soldier; or one M3A1 75 mm howitzer plus crew of three; or 13 troops, equipped.
Flight performance
  Maximum towing speed: 120mph
  Stalling speed: 50mph
  Aspect ratio: 8.21
Tow-planes: C-47; C-46; C-54; A-25; B-25; P-38

A powered Waco CG-4A, the XPG-1

A rare photograph of a Waco CG-4A glider 'mock-up' in a glider and transport mock-up training area. To save the CG-4As wear and tear in the ground phases of airborne training, hundreds of wooden mock-ups were constructed in wooded areas and fields adjacent to airborne divisions. Troops practised loading and lashing $\frac{1}{4}$-ton trucks, artillery and other equipment and ammunition in them. Note the Curtis Commando C-46 mock-up in the background

Water landing a Waco CG-4A at Laurinburg-Maxton Air Base, North Carolina, to test it in water landings and also to determine its floatability, one of the many tests made with this glider to duplicate divers landing situations

exactly like the CG-4A. It performed satisfactorily, but no need ever arose to place it in production.

In all, 13,909 CG-4A's were produced—enough to meet all operational needs. The Ford Motor Company turned out 4,190, while the Northwestern Company of Minneapolis, Minnesota, the second largest producer, built 1,509 gliders. The cost of a CG-4A averaged $18,800.

The AAF built five models of powered gliders (PG), XPG-1, -2, -2A and the PG-2A and XPG-3. One each of the experimental models was built, and ten PG-2A's.

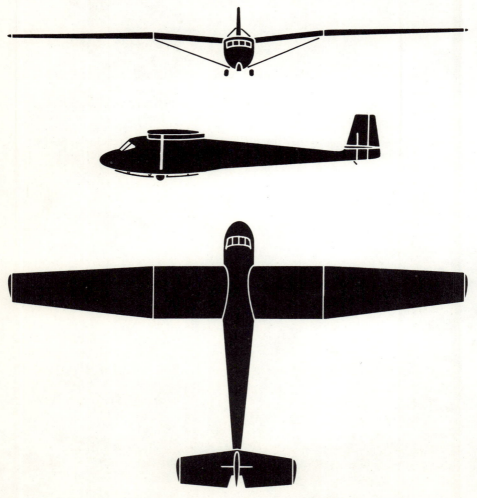

St Louis XCG-5, three-view section

XCG-5

The XCG-5 was developed to serve as a model in the investigation of the effect of light wing loading characteristics. The AAF gave the job to the St. Louis Aircraft Corporation in June 1941, specifying that two glider models should be developed. One was the 8-place XCG-5; the other a 15-place XCG-6.

Early in 1942 the company delivered a static-test model of the XCG-5 to the Materiel Command. Structural tests showed a serious failure at ninety per cent load. Tests on the flight-test model, delivered in October 1942, proved no more successful. Testers found unsatisfactory balance that would have required a complete redesign of the glider if development was to be continued. The AAF decided not to ask the company to undertake the task and terminated the contract. Subsequently, the XCG-6 was also cancelled.

No technical details are available.

XCG-7, -8

To encourage more companies to develop gliders, the AAF awarded a contract to Bowlus Sailplanes, Inc., Los Angeles, California, for two each of an 8-place glider to be known as the XCG-7, and a 15-place glider, to be known as the XCG-8.

The XCG-7 was delivered to Wright Field, where the Materiel Command subjected it to tests during February 1942. It failed the structural test. After repairs, the glider again failed tests.

The company encountered serious problems in producing the larger XCG-8 and prevailed upon the Douglas Aircraft Corporation to render assistance in the project. Despite Douglas's intervention and the enthusiastic endorsement of Dr Wolfgang Klemperer, the former German sailplane and glider designer and pilot (then a Douglas aeronautical engineer) Bowlus made no appreciable progress towards acceptance of the XCG-8 as a production glider. It, too, proved faulty in tests.

The AAF finally concluded that the XCG-7 had proved of 'limited military utility', that the XCG-8 had failed during structural tests, and that there would consequently be no procurement of any Bowlus gliders.

Both gliders were of wood and fabric construction and had a designed towing speed of 120 miles per hour. The XCG-7 was to weigh 5,000lb without load, the XCG-8, 7,450lb.

The XCG-7 flight test-model, which had handled well according to some reports, was sent to the High Voltage Laboratory of the National Bureau of Standards for use in tests in protecting wooden aircraft from lightning. The XCG-8 flight-model was destroyed in a storm at Wilmington, Ohio, in June 1943.

Gull wing St Louis XCG-5

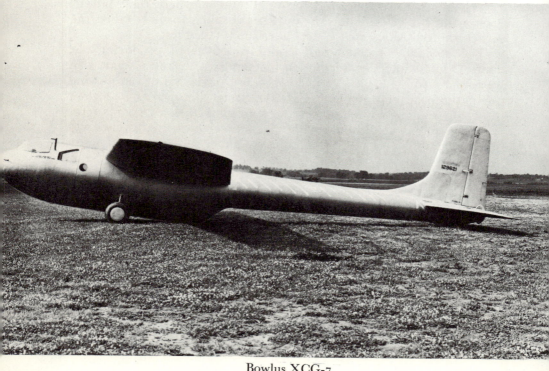

Bowlus XCG-7

Technical Data

Glider Model: XCG-7, CXG-8
Type: transport glider
Crew: pilot, co-pilot
Dimensions
  Wing-span: 80ft 90ft
  Wing area: 600sq ft
    880sq ft
  Fuselage
    Length: 36ft 45ft

Weight
  Total with cargo: 7,000lb
    11,050lb
  Empty: 5,000lb 7,450lb
  Cargo: 2,000lb 3,600lb
Loadings
  XCG-7: 7 troops equipped
  XCG-8: 13 troops equip-
    ped.
Flight performance
  Maximum towing speed:
    120mph

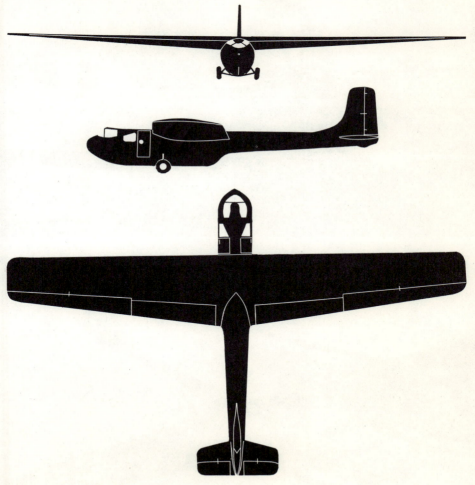

Bowlus XCG-7, three-view section

Bowlus XCG-7, showing nose detail
Bowlus XCG-8
Design concept of the AGA XCG-9. (Note the similarity to the U.S.
Navy's forty-percent scale flight model of its AGA float plane, p. 151)

YCG-10A

Late in 1941 Colonel Frederick R. Dent, Jr., head of the Glider Branch at the Materiel Command, who had just returned from a visit to England to observe Britain's glider activities, expressed the opinion that America must build gliders that could carry substantially more than the CG-4A. If the five U.S. airborne divisions then being organised were to be adequately supplied, they needed gliders that could transport trucks larger than the $\frac{1}{4}$-ton jeep and also large calibre artillery pieces, heavy tonnages of ammunition, and other bulky supplies and equipment.

With this objective in mind the AAF awarded a contract to the Laister Kauffman Aircraft Corporation of St. Louis, Missouri, in April 1942, for the XCG-10, a 30-place glider. Three were to be built, constructed from wood so far as was practical.

In October the company delivered a static-test model to Wright Field. (By then Waco had made substantial progress on the large XCG-13, a glider with characteristics comparable to those specified for the XCG-10.)

When the Waco XCG-13 was approved for production, the AAF dropped work on the XCG-10 and asked Laister Kauffman to develop a somewhat larger glider, the XCG-10A. The XCG-10A specifications called for a troop/cargo glider that would transport a combat load of 8,000lb; a gross weight of 15,980lb. Its wing-span was to be 105 feet and the fuselage 68.5 feet in length. Air speed was set at 150 miles per hour. This was an increase over the 120 miles per hour established for earlier models, designed to take advantage of faster C-46 and C-54 tow aeroplanes, which had become available for airborne operations. On 30 April 1944 the company delivered a flight-model to the Clinton County field. It had the distinction of being the only large wooden aircraft to pass military testing successfully in many years.

The XCG-10A was a high-wing, full cantilever, monoplane glider. Tail surfaces were supported by a boom attached to the upper rear portion of the fuselage. It had a tricycle landing gear with a retractable nose wheel. Spoilers on the upper surface of the wing were operated manually by a lever in the cockpit. Slotted flaps covered one half of the wing length and were operated hydraulically. The glider had dual control; the pilots sat side by side. To comply with the original contract, the entire craft, with the exception of fittings, was of moulded plywood.

The outstanding feature of the glider was its enormous cargo compartment, 30 feet long, which extended from the pilot's compartment to about four feet aft of the rear edge of the wing. The exterior of the cargo section cleared the ground by only 20 inches. It had

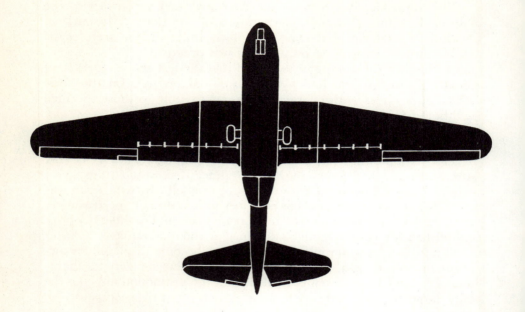

Laister-Kaufmann YCG-10A, three-view section

Laister-Kaufmann YCG-10A, Trojan Horse America's largest all-wood glider, and the pride of her glider fleet

261099

The Laister-Kaufmann YCG-10A was loaded from the rear

Snead XCG-11 wind-tunnel test model

Read-York, XCG-12 wind-tunnel test model

clamshell doors and a ramp that could be lowered at the rear of the compartment to load a 2½-ton truck.

Large though the glider was, it proved suitable for 'snatch' pickups. These were in fact accomplished by the B-17 bomber and the C-54 transport airplane.

There was pressure for the production of large gliders as quickly as possible. Thus, although the XCG-10A had not been accepted as a standard piece of equipment, the AAF negotiated a production contract with Laister Kauffman in August 1942 for ten YCG-10A's, the designation of the production model, which the company built by 1945.

In early 1945, William S Knudsen, head of the War Production Board, asked Mr Jack Laister to Washington. There he grilled Mr Laister on technical details and operational characteristics of the company's glider as well as its production qualifications. Concluding the conference, Mr Knudsen stated he was entirely satisfied with the YCG-10 programme.

Shortly afterwards, the company received instructions to gear up for the production of 1,000 CG-10As. These gliders were to participate in the invasion of Japan. To be built in St Louis, they were to then be shipped by barge down the Mississippi and at New Orleans loaded on freighters and shipped via the Panama Canal to islands in the Pacific to be readied for the assault.

This programme was not immediately terminated when the war against Japan ended as were other glider contracts, a testimony to the confidence the AAF had in the company and the transport. Manufacturing continued into 1946 before the contract was closed.

Technical Data

Glider Model: XCG-10A, YCG-10A
Type: transport glider
Crew: pilot, co-pilot
Dimensions
  Wing-span: 105ft
  Wing area: 1180sq ft
  Fuselage
    Length: 67ft
    Height: 26.3ft
  Cargo compartment
    Length: 30ft
    Width: 8.5ft
    Height: 6.7ft
Weight
  Total with cargo: 23,000lb
  Empty: 12,150lb
  Cargo: 10,850lb

Loadings
  2½-ton truck; two 105 mm howitzers (M2); one M1, 155 mm Howitzer; one M2 howitzer and a ¼-ton 4 × 4 truck; or 40 troops, equipped.
Flight performance
  Maximum airspeed: 180mph
  Maximum airspeed with flaps: 140mph
  Stalling speed
    Flaps up: 75mph
    Flaps down: 70mph
  Aspect ratio: 8.15
Tow-planes: C-47; C-46; C-54

CG-13A

Because of the success of the Waco Company with the CG-4A the AAF decided to apply Waco's experience to designing and developing a glider of larger capacity. As a result, on 23 September 1942 they were asked to develop the XCG-13, a 30-place transport glider with a towing speed of 175 miles per hour at 12,000 feet altitude, a gross weight of 15,000 pounds and a useful military load of 8,000lb.

Testing began in March of the first XCG-13 prototype, at Wright Field. The glider passed preliminary tests successfully, with a few modifications.

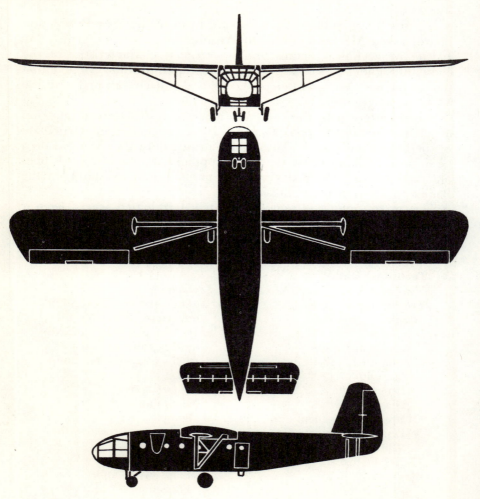

Waco CG-13A, three-view section

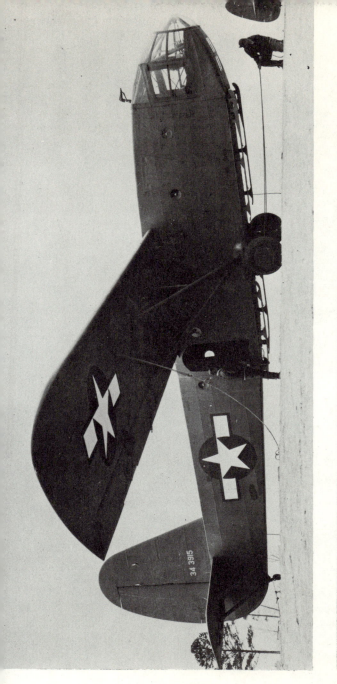

Waco CG-13 with tail-wheel landing gear

Waco CG-13A with nose-wheel (tricycle) landing gear

Loading a tracked weapons-carrier in a CG-13A

Interior of a Waco CG-13A

On 7 July, after a tornado had wrecked the second flight-test model, a static-test model was tested and approved. By the end of the summer of 1943 the AAF had the first large glider ready for production. Since actual production orders went out before tests were completed, the early production models were designated the YCG-13A. Later in full production the glider became the CG-13A.

The fuselage framework was made of welded steel tubing covered with fabric. Wings were of wood and externally braced. Flaps were hydraulically operated. Like that of the CG-4A, the nose of the CG-13A was hinged at the top and could be elevated by means of a pair of hydraulic actuating cylinders. Ramps were then dropped and vehicles driven into the interior. It was possible to release four aerial delivery containers or parapacks through doors at the rear of the cargo compartment while the glider was in flight. Pilots sat side by side at dual controls. Despite the size of this glider, it could be picked up with ease by a tow-craft in the glider-snatch technique developed midway through the war.

The glider was given a clear approval, and went into production. Ford produced eighty-five, Northwestern forty-seven.

Technical Data

Glider Model: CG-13A
Type: transport glider
Crew: pilot, co-pilot
Dimensions
  Wing-span: 86ft
  Wing area: 873sq ft
  Fuselage
    Length: 54ft
    Height: 20ft
  Cargo compartment
    Length: 24ft
    Width: 7.5ft
    Height: 6ft
Weight
  Total with cargo: 18,900lb
  Empty: 8,700lb
  Cargo: 10,200lb

Loadings
  One M2 105 mm howitzer, one $\frac{1}{4}$-ton 4 × 4 truck, ammunition, and gun crew; or one $1\frac{1}{2}$-ton 6 × 6 truck; or 40 troops, equipped.
Flight performance
  Maximum airspeed: 195mph
  Maximum airspeed with flaps: 150mph
  Towing speed: 135mph
  Stalling speed:
    Flaps up: 83mph
    Flaps down: 79mph
  Aspect ratio: 8.41

Tow-planes: C-47; C-46; C-54, B-17, B-24

XCG-14, 14A

The XCG-14 was the last of the 15-place gliders produced by the AAF. It was designed and developed to meet new concepts in the tactical use of gliders. Faster and more powerful tow-planes, such as the C-54, were being produced and this meant that the slower transport gliders would no longer be suitable for tow by planes such as the C-54. Also, some glider proponents in the AAF saw gliders as fighter air-support vehicles, ferrying aircraft components, built-in workshops or other facilities, to be towed by fighters in close support of fighter bases in theatres of air operations. The Germans were already doing this, particularly with their Go 242's. Finally, one school of opinion felt a glider was needed that could be towed to a high-altitude release point beyond the reach of enemy sensors, for

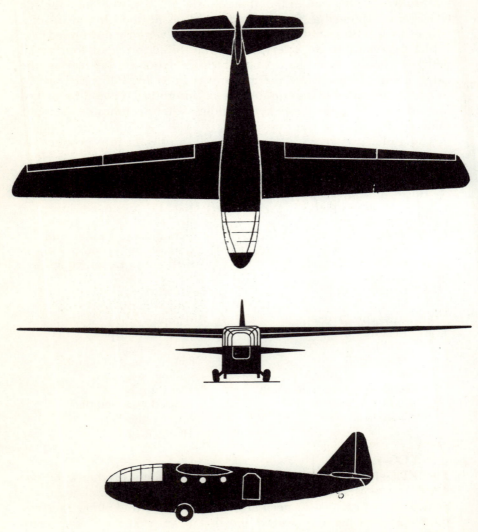

Chase XCG-14, three-view section

missions requiring great secrecy or a high degree of tactical or strategic surprise. Such a glider must withstand stresses not expected of existing gliders.

The glider produced to meet these requirements was the XCG-14. The AAF negotiated a contract with the Chase Aircraft Company of New York on 30 October 1943. The Russian-born engineer and architect Michael Stroukoff, builder of railroads, bridges and theatres and part owner of Chase, designed the XCG-14, applying his knowledge of hydrodynamics to the problem of obtaining the highest performance from a wing. The result was a surprisingly good glider with a high, full cantilever wing and such a high aspect ratio as had not been recorded up to then in the files of the U.S. National Advisory Committee on Aeronautics, the repository for all airfoil design.

The XCG-14 was built in the loft of an old building in lower Manhattan, then disassembled, moved out in sections to a garage in the Bronx near Bailey Avenue, and there reassembled.

Technical Data

Glider Model(s): XCG-14, XCG-14A
Type: high-speed transport glider
Crew: pilot, co-pilot
Dimensions
  Wing-span: 71.8ft, 86.25ft
  Wing area: 507sq ft, 706.5sq ft
  Fuselage
    Length: 42.8ft, 55ft
    Height (approx.): 6.8ft
  Cargo compartment
    Length: 24ft, 38ft
    Width: 5.5ft
    Height: 5.8ft
Tow-planes: P-38 or other fighter aircraft

Weight
  Total with cargo 7,605lb 15,000
  Empty: 3,237lb, 7,500
  Cargo: 4,368lb, 8,000
Loadings
  One $\frac{1}{4}$-ton 4 × 4 truck plus three soldiers; one M3A1 75 mm howitzer plus crew or 15 troops, equipped; or 24 troops, equipped
Flight performance
  Maximum towing speed: 170mph
  Stalling speed
    Flaps down: 60mph
  Aspect ratio: 10.18

The XCG-14 had a maximum designed airspeed of 200 miles per hour. The fuselage had a natural marine plywood skin and was wood braced, as were the wing and tail. Its rich, polished mahogany surface made it a superb product of the wood-worker's art, but it was soon painted over with aluminium paint. The rear part of the fuselage pivoted upward about a horizontal hinge, to provide access to the cargo compartment, The glider had a fixed main landing gear, retractable nose, manually-operated wing flaps, and dual control. It had a large plexiglass 'greenhouse' nose, giving an unexcelled field of vision to the pilots, (although it was later found that some pilots experienced optical distortion, a result of light rays being bent by the moulded glass).

The second, modified, model was designated the XCG-14A. It will be noted in the photograph, that although the wing was the same, other alterations were substantial, such as the increase in the number of passengers from fourteen to twenty-four fully-equipped troops. The moulded glass was replaced by flat glass panels, and the cargo compartment was made more commodious. The tail in the XCG-14A was also raised to permit the cargo compartment to be opened for loading purposes.

Both models of the glider proved satisfactory in tests. The XCG-14A was at one time towed at 275 miles per hour by a Republic P-47 (Thunderbolt) fighter. These two gliders and other gliders produced by Chase came to be known as 'Avitrucs'.

CG-15A

By the autumn of 1943 enough data had been collected to indicate that it was now time either to make major modifications in the successful CG-4A, or to launch into the design and development of a new glider with comparable cargo capacity but with better flying characteristics. Thousands of CG-4A's had flown in training, manoeuvres and operations, towed by many different planes and in a variety of weather conditions. In preparation for airborne operations in the Mediterranean theatre, and for the cross-channel invasion, a build-up of glider forces was under way in Africa and in England. The decision was now made to build a new glider, the XCG-15, incorporating the needed changes.

Major Floyd Sweet, a design and development engineer and chief test pilot who had become head of the Glider Branch when Colonel Dent was assigned to a bomber command overseas, became project engineer for the XCG-15. Conferring with Francis Acier, the chief aeronautical engineer of Waco (who had been instrumental in the design of the CG-4A), Sweet soon made a few, but important, modifications to the CG-4A design to produce one for the XCG-15, which was not markedly different from the CG-4A in basic design. Consequently, the transition to the XCG-15 by companies already producing the CG-4A was relatively simple to accomplish.

On 14 October 1943 Waco changed to construction of the CG-15A. The new glider had a forty per cent shorter wing-span than the CG-4A; its most distinguishing characteristic. Other differences included the addition of flaps and new ailerons, crash protection for passengers and crew, a somewhat higher towing speed, improved landing gear, and better visibility for the pilot. Although the glider

Chase XCG-14

Chase XCG-14A

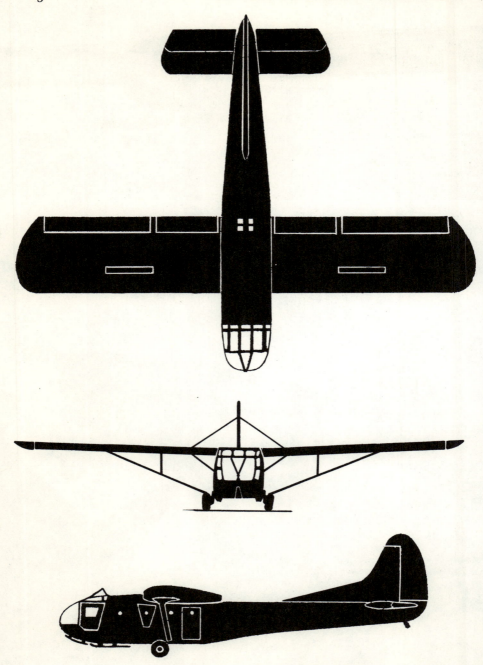

Waco CG-15A, three-view section

was 400lb heavier than the CG-4A, it carried some 500lb more in men or cargo. Because the CG-15 had flaps, whereas the CG-4A did not, it had a higher sink rate when the flaps were used.

Three months after the contract for production gliders was signed, the first of the CG-15A's was delivered to Wright Field.

Technical Data

Glider Model: CG-15A
Type: transport glider
Crew: pilot, co-pilot
Dimensions
  Wing-span: 62.1ft
  Wing area: 623sq ft
  Fuselage
    Length: 48.8ft
    Height: 12.7ft
  Cargo compartment
    Length: 13.1ft
    Width: 5.9ft
    Height: 5.5ft
Weight
  Total with cargo: 8,000lb
  Empty: 4,000lb
  Cargo: 4,000lb

Loadings
  One $\frac{1}{4}$-ton 4 × 4 truck, driver and two other soldiers; one M3A1 105 mm howitzer with crew; or 13 troops, equipped.
Flight performance
  Maximum airspeed: 180mph
  Maximum airspeed with flaps: 100mph
  Stalling speed
    Flaps up: 62mph
    Flaps down: 53mph
  Aspect ratio: 6.21
Tow-planes: C-47; C-46; C-54; A-25; B-25; P-38

XCG-16

The XCG-16 was an interesting departure from the single-fuselage design which had been common to American gliders. It also introduced the twin boom. In it the trend towards better aerodynamic characteristics for transport gliders could be seen that was to reach its apogee in the XG-20, a post-war development. It is worth noting that the XCG-16 had some of the same aerodynamic design elements as the German *Mammut*.

The story of its development is extraordinary. In February 1942 William Hawley Bowlus of Bowlus Sailplanes began the design and construction of a flying wing glider. A half-size prototype of the glider was completed later that year, and in October, Mr. Bowlus and an associate, Mr. Albert Criz, began a campaign to secure a government contract. They organized the Airborne Transport Company in Los Angeles, California, which finally became the General Airborne Transport Company.

An inspection of Airborne Transport's facilities, disclosed that the 'factory' was a small store building formerly used as a dry cleaning shop; just large enough for the half-sized glider they had constructed to be fitted into the building sideways.

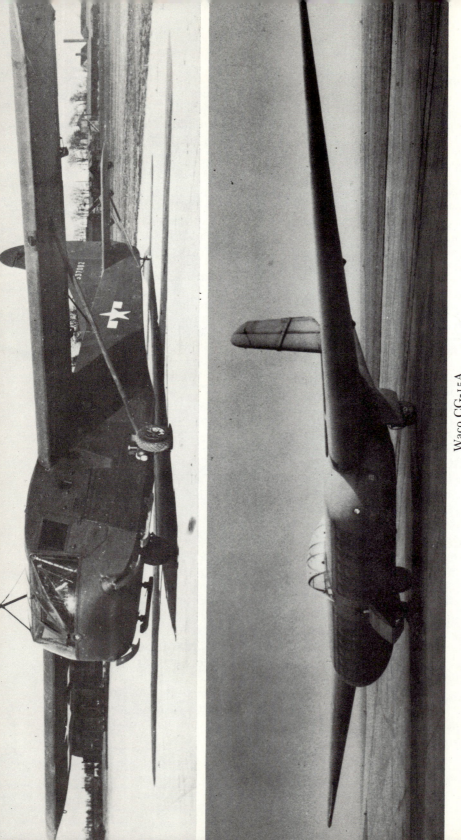

Waco CG-15A
General Airborne XCG-16

Next, the Company launched into the construction of a full-scale model, looking for support in Washington. They were stimulated by self deception, or possible political support, into the belief that a contract for 1,000 of their gliders was in the offing.

After completing the glider, Airborne Transport Company offered it to Wright Field for test and evaluation. Meanwhile the company conducted its own tests. On 11 September 1943 Richard duPont,

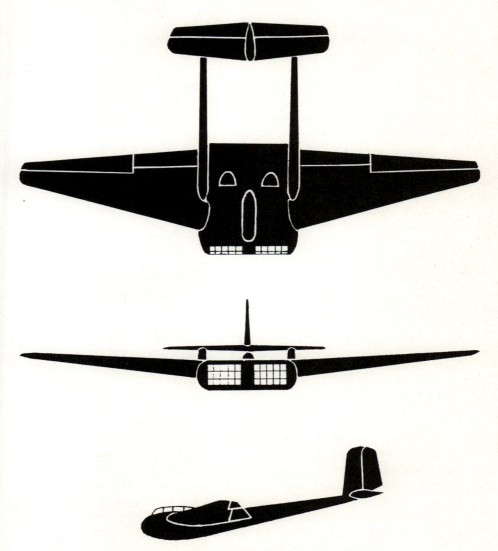

General Airborne XCG-16, three-view section

the glider specialist on the staff of the Chief of Staff of the Air Force, and Colonel Ernest Gabel of the same office were killed when the MC-1 crashed at March Field, California. Mr. Bowlus, without authority from military officials, had arranged for a test flight. The glider took off with some passengers, and loaded with bags of lead shot or sand to bring the load up to capacity. Unfortunately no one had the forethought to lash in the dead weight bags, and they shifted in the turbulence. The glider began 'porpoising', endangering the tow-plane. The tow-plane's pilot cut the MC-1 loose. By this time the glider was so off balance that it was uncontrollable, and went into a dive. Mr Bowlus and one other passenger managed to parachute to safety. All others were killed.

This tragedy did not deter the company, and a contract was approved on 13 November. They finally delivered one glider, some six months later than promised and at three times the original cost estimate. This glider became the XCG-16.

Technical Data

Glider Model: XCG-16
Type: transport glider
Crew: pilot, co-pilot
Dimensions
  Wing-span: 91.8ft
  Wing area: 1140sq ft
  Fuselage
   Length: 48.3ft
   Height: 18.3ft
  Cargo compartment
   Length: 15ft
   Width: 7ft
   Height: 5ft
Weight
  Total with cargo: 19,580lb
  Empty: 9,500lb
  Cargo: 10,080lb

Loadings
  Two M2 105 mm howitz-ers; or one M2 105 mm howitzer, and one $\frac{1}{4}$-ton 4 × 4 truck with gun crew; or 42 troops, equipped.
Flight performance
  Maximum airspeed: 220mph
  Maximum airspeed with flaps: 120mph
  Stalling speed
   Flaps up: 62mph
   Flaps down: 58mph
  Aspect ratio: 7.4
Tow-planes: C-47, C-46, C-60

It was a high wing, cantilever monoplane with twin booms to support the empennage. Unique from an aerodynamic standpoint was the airfoil-shaped fuselage between the booms, looking much like the Brunelli aeroplane introduced in the early 1930s. The front of the wing on each side of the loading nacelle opened like a jaw, the top swinging about horizontal hinges along the leading edge of the airfoil, the bottom swinging on hinges on the bottom of the fuselage to rest on the ground and form a loading ramp. The glider had dual control and the pilots sat in tandem. Landing gear was retractable. The outer

Unloading the General Airborne XCG-16

A rare photograph of two Douglas C-47s in tandem towing an XCG-17, the glider counterpart of the Douglas C-47, in experimental towing tests

wing panels had slotted wing-flaps, and the centre section of the fuse-lage also had a split flap. The flaps were actuated by electrical power. The glider was constructed largely of plywood; movable surfaces, such as flaps, were covered with fabric. Because the cargo area tapered to zero at the rear, the seats at the rear of the fuselage allowed little head-room for passengers.

The glider was tested at the Clinton Army Air Field and at Orlando, Florida, by the AAF Board. It concluded that the glider had inade-quate crash protection, unsatisfactory loading ramps, insufficient personnel exits, awkward location of flight equipment, critical lateral loading and restricted pilot visibility. The contract was terminated on 30th November 1944.

XCG-17

The XCG-17 represents one of the later, although certainly more innovative developments in wartime gliders. It arose from need.

In the fall of 1944 the AAF was faced with the problem of delivering large quantities of supplies from India to China. This meant flying over the so-called 'hump' in Burma. Since sufficient cargo planes were not available for the task, it was proposed that transport gliders might be used to improve the supply situation, and glider development took a unique turn. The AAF decided to see if the C-47 aeroplane, the reliable workhorse of the military and civilian transport services, could be saddled with yet another task.

With reasonable modifications it was found possible to produce a glider version of the C-47 that, towed by a C-54 aeroplane, could carry up to 15,000lb of cargo.

To attain the maximum cargo capacity, the C-47 was stripped of radio and navigator's equipment, and the space turned into a part of the cargo compartment. Bulkheads were removed, creating a space 30.4 feet long. Engines were also removed and the nacelles covered with spun-aluminium caps. Wing outer panels and the vacant nacelles were converted into fuel storage tanks to carry fuel as cargo. By these various actions cargo capacity was ultimately boosted to 15,000 pounds to make the XCG-17 America's largest cargo-carrying glider of the war.

The man-hours needed to make the conversion proved surprisingly few for the results achieved, and later tests confirmed the feasibility of converting a C-47 into an efficient cargo glider. It was determined that the XCG-17 could be reconverted to a C-47 in equally few hours.

However, while development and testing were taking place, the supply situation in the China-Burma-India theatre improved, and there was no longer a requirement for the conversion of substantial numbers of C-47's.

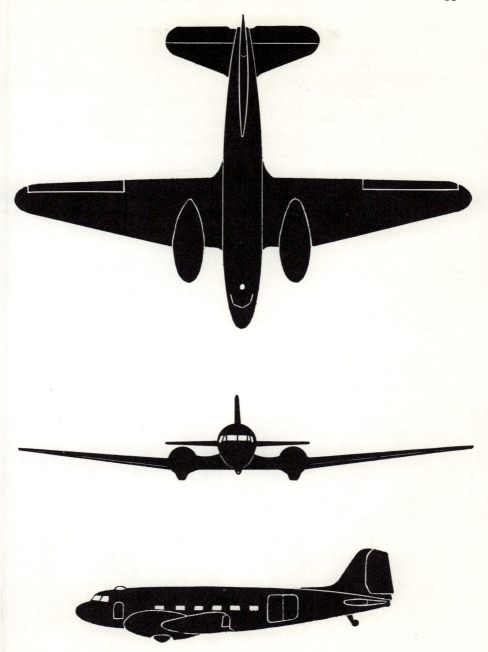

XCG-17, three-view section

XCG-17 glider, a converted Douglas DC-3

Chase XCG-18A

Technical Data

Glider Model: XCG-17
Type: transport glider
Crew: pilot, co-pilot
Dimensions
   Wing-span: 95ft
   Wing area: 987sq ft
   Fuselage
     Length: 63.8ft
     Height: 17ft
   Cargo compartment
     Length: 30.3ft
     Width: 8ft
     Height: 6ft
Weight
   Total with cargo: 26,000lb
   Empty: 11,000lb
   Cargo: 15,000lb

Loadings
   Three $\frac{1}{4}$-ton 4 × 4 trucks
   plus drivers; miscellaneous
   cargo including fuels; or
   27 troops, equipped.
Flight performance
   Maximum airspeed:
   190mph
   Maximum airspeed with
   flaps: 112mph
   Stalling speed
     Flaps up: 75mph
     Flaps down: 66mph
   Aspect ratio: 9.15
Tow-planes: C-54, two C-47's in
   tandem tow.

XCG-18A

As the war progressed most of the characteristics for military gliders became outdated. Moreover, the Deputy Chief of Air Staff declared that 'all present types of gliders are considered to be obsolescent, because they deteriorate rapidly and are inflexible in that they can be used only as gliders'. This set the stage for a new U.S. glider programme; although its full implementation took effect only after the end of the war.

In the spring of 1945, two new gliders were proposed, one to have a useful military load of 8,000lb and a cargo compartment twenty-four feet long; the second to have a 16,000lb load capacity with a cargo compartment thirty feet long. Up to that time the largest gun a U.S. glider could carry was the 75 mm howitzer, too small a weapon for expanding airborne needs. The weight of the equipment a glider could transport was henceforth to be the governing factor, rather than the number of troops it could carry. Also important in the design of gliders was to be the stipulation that they could readily be converted into powered aircraft with the addition of engines.

Chase Aircraft received a contract in January 1946 for the manufacture of the XCG-18A which although it looked strikingly similar to the XCG-14A, was much different in that it had an all-metal steel-framed fuselage covered by light sheet aluminium. Other features were an aluminium-covered wing and tail surface, tricycle landing gear and a retractable nose wheel.

Loading and unloading were accomplished by raising the entire

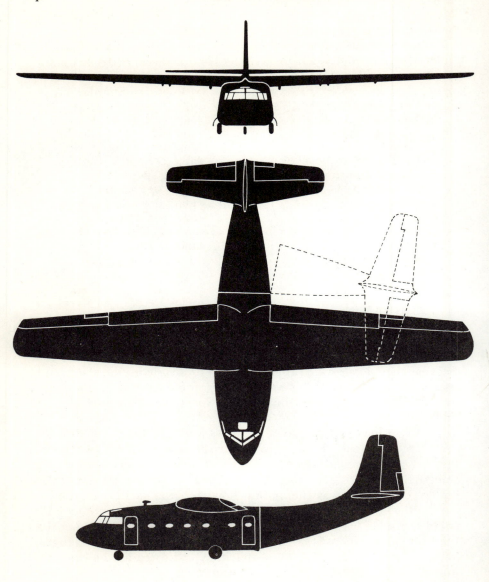

Douglas XCG-19 design concept

tail section, which afforded an opening 7.7 feet high by 6.5 feet in width. It had a designed top speed of 180 miles per hour.

Because specifications were changed midway in production, the glider was not completed until 1948. The designer, Mr. Stroukoff, demonstrated his axiom that to be successful as an aircraft an aeroplane must be a good glider first; for he added two Wright R-1850 engines and provided the Air Force with a sister ship (the XC-122) to the XCG-18A that could both carry cargo and act as a tow-ship.

The reliable XCG-18A was later transformed into the powered C-122.

Technical Data

Glider Model: XCG-18A
Type: all-metal transport glider
Crew: pilot, co-pilot
Dimensions
  Wing-span: 71.8 ft
  Wing area: 507sq ft
  Fuselage
   Length: 53ft
  Cargo compartment
   Length: 24ft

Weight
  Total with cargo: 22,700lb
  Empty: 14,700lb
  Cargo: 8,000lb
Loadings
  30 troops, equipped, or troops and cargo to a maximum load of 14,700lb

XCG-19

Because of the interest of the AAF in the all-metal glider, it determined to construct an 8,000 pound metal monocoque glider, essentially the same design as the XCG-18. Whereas in the XCG-18 the stress was taken by the steel-tubing framework, and the sheet aluminum was used as fairing only, in the XCG-19 the aluminum covering of the fuselage was structured to take the stress.

Bell, Douglas and Hughes responded to the solicitations for proposals. Douglas received the contract in 1946 and by March of 1947 had a mock up 60 percent complete. However, because of Defense Department budget limitations imposed on the Air Force that year, the Air Force determined to cancel either the XCG-18 or the XCG-19. Since the former was near completion, the Air Force decided to cancel the Douglas contract for the XCG-19.

The XCG-19 was considered a light assault cargo glider. It had an 85-foot wing-span and was 61 feet long. Its cargo compartment measured 24.7 feet by 7.7 by 6.5. It loaded from the rear with the cargo doors opening out and down. Its loaded weight was 14,380 pounds and it carried 8,000 pounds of cargo.

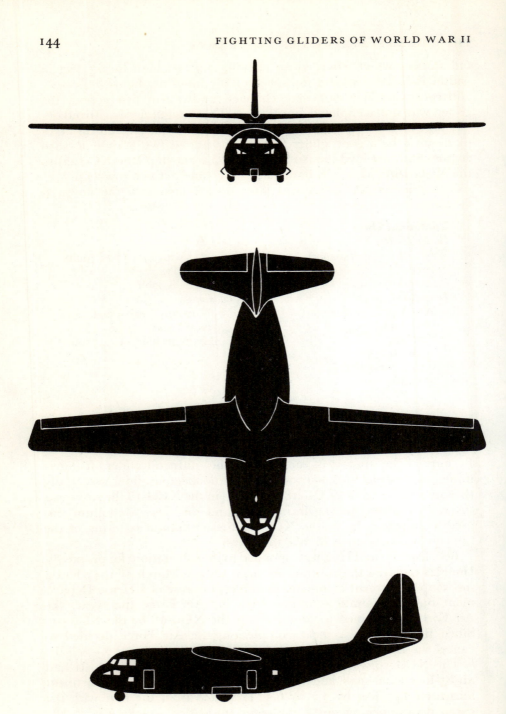

Chase XCG-20

XCG-20

An unusually symmetrical aircraft, the XCG-20 was a high-wing glider of all-metal monocoque construction, equipped with fully-retractable tricycle landing gear and hydraulically-operated slot flaps. The hydraulic pump was electrically driven, the power plant supplied by a petrol-driven auxiliary motor. It met the requirement for a glider that could carry a useful military load of 16,000lb. It had a combination door and loading ramp at the rear of the cargo compartment that provided easy access for loading bulky cargo. It could seat sixty troops or accommodate fifty litter-patients.

Chase Aircraft received the contract to manufacture the all-metal XCG-20 on 2 December 1946.

In the tradition of the XCG-18A XC-122, the XCG-20's sister ship with reciprocating engines was the XC-123. Surprisingly in 1951 the glider was equipped with two twin J-47 jet pods 'borrowed' from a B-47. It was flown in and out of short fields and had a maximum speed of over 500 miles per hour and became America's first jet transport.

Technical Data

Glider Model: XCG-20
Type: Heavy transport glider
Crew: pilot, co-pilot, crew-chief/mechanic
Dimensions
  Wing-span: 110ft
  Wing area: 880sq ft
  Fuselage
    Length: 77ft
  Cargo compartment
    Length: 30ft
    Width: 12ft
    Height: 10ft

Weight
  Cargo: 16,000lb
Loadings
  60 troops, equipped; 50 litter-patients; or trucks, tanks and guns to the load limit of 16,000lb.

XFG-1

In October 1943 the AAF wished to test the feasibility of extending the range of cargo and bombardment aircraft through the use of a trailing glider carrying fuel. The Cornelius Aircraft Corporation of Dayton, Ohio developed the glider, which was to test an unusual aerodynamic configuration that might also be used for a fighter plane.

The glider, decidedly non-conventional in design, had forward-swept wings, and no horizontal tail surface as found in conventional airplanes. It carried 764 gallons of fuel and had a total loaded weight of 8,000 pounds. The wings swept forward fifteen degrees at 25 per cent chord line position. The undercarriage could be jettisoned.

Chase XCG-20 from which aircraft industry borrowed many design innovations, which were incorporated into some of America's most advanced aircraft

Cornelius XFG-1 fuel glider

The Sparton Aircraft Company of Tulsa, Oklahoma, constructed the glider under a subcontract. Wind tunnel and structural tests were made during the summer of 1944, and on 11 October of that year the XFG-1 made its first flight test. Later that year a Sparton test pilot checking for spin recovery was unable to bring the glider out of a spin and was killed in the ensuing crash.

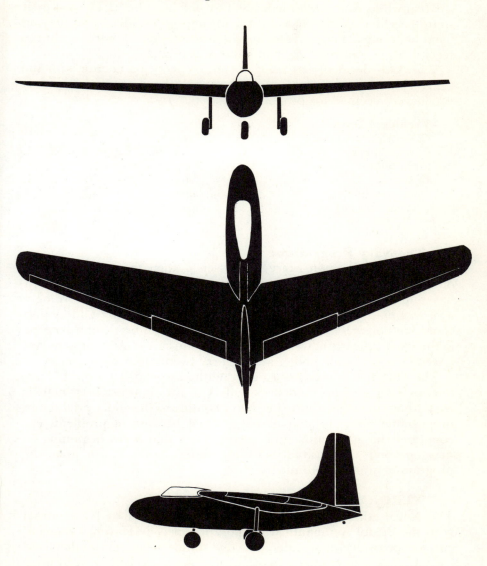

Cornelius XFG-1 fuel glider, three-view section

Captain Adam J. Stolzenberger took charge of the project of build-ing a quarter-scale, free-flight, radio-controlled model. It was built at Wright Field and taken to the Naval Air Station at Lakehurst, New Jersey, where a Navy blimp lifted it to the desired release altitude. The model was put into a spin and successfully recovered by opening a safety parachute.

Meanwhile, a new test model XFG-1 had been built. The test pilot spun the glider on the first test, recovering successfully by employing what he termed 'a critical sequence and trimming of controls'. On the second test a spin-recovery parachute was used.

The AAF decided that using a spin-recovery parachute with the XFG-1 was the only effective way to recover the glider from a spin. It was never accepted for production.

Technical Data

Glider Model: XFG-1
Type: fuel glider
Crew: pilot
Dimensions
  Wing-span: 54ft
  Wing area: 356sq ft

Weight
  Total with cargo: 8,000lb
  Empty: 3,362lb
  Cargo: 4,638lb
Loadings
  764 gallons of fuel

The Navy Programme

In April 1941 Captain Marc A. Mitscher, then the Assistant Chief of the Bureau of Naval Aeronautics, directed the production of a 'personnel and equipment' carrying glider for the Navy. Accordingly a programme was developed to produce two float-wing gliders that could land on water. It was hoped that large numbers could be used in the Pacific theatre of war. One glider was to carry twelve passengers; a second, a twin-hull model, was to carry twenty-four passengers.

The Marine Corps expressed great enthusiasm for the project. They foresaw that gliders could prove effective attack transports in their island-hopping campaigns. The Navy continued the glider production programme until the end of 1943. Then because of problems en-countered in production and uncertainties that were beginning to develop about the feasibility of using gliders in the Pacific area, the programme was discontinued.

XLRQ-1*

The Naval Aircraft Factory at Philadelphia negotiated a contract with the Bristol Aeronautical Corporation of New Haven, Connecti-cut, for the twelve-man glider. The first static test model was delivered

* X (experimental); L (glider); R (transport); the fourth letter designated the manufacturer, e.g. N (Naval Aircraft factory).

Navy Bristol XLRQ-1, four view section

in October 1942 under the designation XLRQ-1. After static tests, controls and instruments were installed and the glider was prepared for limited test flights. These took place during January 1943. The J2F-5 and the PBY-5A were used as tow-planes.

A flight-test model was delivered on 5 May 1943. This glider had a tricycle landing gear and a wheel control system for the pilot. Testing continued into the latter part of the year.

The XLRQ-1 had excellent visibility for passengers and crew. A transparent panelled plexiglass cover extended from the nose to a point midway in the fuselage.

Only two gliders were constructed, although at one point in the early stages, optimistic supporters had talked in terms of producing 12,000 of them. The twin-hull, 24-place model was never built.

Technical Data

Glider Model: XLRQ-1	*Dimensions*
Type: amphibious transport glider	Wing-span: 71ft
	Wing area: 500sq ft
Crew: pilot, co-pilot	Fuselage
Loading: 10 equipped marines	Length: 43.5ft
Tow-planes: J2F-5 and PBY-5A	Height: 16ft

XLRA-1, -2

The Navy contracted with Allied Aviation of Baltimore, Maryland for XLRA float wing gliders. In configuration and construction, they were similar to the XLRQ-1, differing primarily in landing gear. The XLRA-1 had a dual centre wheel and wing tip skids. The XLRA-2 had a conventional, two wheel, but jettisonable landing gear.

Each were primarily of wood construction with fuselage and wing skin of impregnated plywood and a two-step planing hull. Wingspans were 70.5 feet and fuselage lengths 40 feet.

Although the Navy contracted for 100 LRA's, contracts were cancelled before any but the prototypes were built.

XLRG-1; XLRH-1

Two contracts were let for 24-place gliders. Prior to letting contracts for either of these gliders the Navy let a contract to the AGA Aviation Corporation of Willow Grove, Pennsylvania, for the construction of a 40 percent scale model of what was later to become the XLRG-1. In exactly thirty-five days after getting the contract AGA produced the glider and delivered it to Philadelphia. There the head of the glider development programme, Captain R. S. Barnaby, U.S.N., flew the glider successfully on a number of test flights.

Navy Bristol XLRQ-1
Navy AGA float glider, forty-percent scale model
Navy Allied XLRN-1

On 23rd December 1941 the Navy awarded a contract to AGA, later to become G & A Aircraft Inc., for the construction of the XLRG-1. This configuration was to be of 'twin-float' design. Each float was to be designed to carry five equipped men. The centre nacelle was to carry the pilot, a co-pilot and twelve men.

Shortly thereafter, the Navy negotiated a contract with Snead and Company to produce a 'twin-hull' model, the XLRH-1. Although the Navy had sufficient confidence in this model to contract for the production of fifty articles, it terminated the contract with Snead and AGA before either prototype was completed.

XLRN-1

Designed and built in tight secrecy at the Naval Aircraft Factory, Johnsonville, Pennsylvania, the all-wood XLRN-1 was one of America's two largest gliders and least known. It had a 110-foot wingspan and a rated load of 18,000 pounds. Two documents differ on loaded weights, one indicating 33,160, the other, 37,764 pounds. Its overload weight was 40,000 pounds.

Its contemplated use was as a troop transport, a 3,000-gallon fuel glider, and most spectacularly as a bomb-glider to fly into the mouth of a German submarine pen and explode on impact. For this last use it had a television-like sensor in the nose.

It was test flown many times and reported as heavy at the controls. A Navy four-engined Douglas R5D towed the XLRN-1.

Technical Data

Glider Model: XLRN-1
Type: fuel, transport, glide bomb
Crew: pilot, co-pilot
Dimensions
  Wing-span: 110ft
  Wing area: 1,200sq ft
  Length: 67.5ft
Weight
  Total with cargo: 33,160/ 37,764lb
  Empty: 15,160/19,764lb
  Cargo: 18,000/19,764lb

Loadings
  80 troops equipped; 3,000 gal fuel; high explosives
Flight performance
  Towing speed: 180mph
Tow-plane: R5D

Bomb-Glider

The Navy also had a bomb-glider development programme. It relied on existing air frames using Taylorcraft, Piper and Aeronca aeroplanes, replacing engines with extended nose nacelles and a nose wheel thus converting them to tricycle landing aircraft. Equipped

Navy bomb glider

Timm XAG-2 assault glider

with TV and radar, these systems proved highly reliable during extensive testing. They never were used operationally, however.

Other Developments

In addition to the experimental and production gliders already discussed, the AAF signed contracts for the XCG-9, -11, -12, -19 and the XAG-1 and -2, which reached various stages of completion but were not accepted. Most contracts were cancelled. Some wind-tunnel models were built.

Moreover, glider production brought with it the need for investigation into which related, innovative, technical developments or ideas, would make gliders more effective.

Training Gliders

Less well-known than the transport glider programme, but none the less important, was the production of the single-place, two-place, and three-place training gliders, designated XTG's and TG's. Many companies participated in the design and manufacture of the ten different training glider models. Of these, seven went into production, and 1,210 of them, were built.

Powered Gliders

The AAF experimented with a number of twin-engine CG-4A gliders. Originally many AAF leaders had in mind that gliders were to be expendable, one-mission, aircraft. Later manoeuvres and operations proved gliders to be durable beyond expectation, and this viewpoint changed. Also, it was considered poor economics to build gliders as large as were being constructed, and then to use them for just a single mission. For this reason, and to have an aircraft able to carry bulky loads over short distances, the idea was conceived of placing a 'package' engine installation in the gliders. This installation was to be so designed that the glider could be converted to a powered aircraft within a few hours. Power in a glider would also be used to assist in take-offs, to extend gliding range, and to provide a means of recovering a glider after it had landed and returning it to friendly lines.

Three powered gliders were developed. The CG-4A powered by two 125 h.p. Franklin engines became the XPG-1. The CG-4A powered by two 175 h.p. Ranger engines became the XPG-2. The CG-15A was powered by two Jacobs R-755-9 engines. All tested satisfactorily. However, it was determined that there would be no tactical use for them, although if the occasion arose they were available for production.

Bomb-Gliders

In 1942 the AAF procured ten XBG-1 bomb-gliders. These gliders were to have an explosive warhead, and be released from under the wing of a bomber. An operator in the bomber was to direct the glider to its target by radio control. They never became operational.

Assault-Glider

An idea that tantalised the Army ground forces but drew heavy fire from the AAF was that of an assault glider; an armed glider suitable for landing on fields that had not yet been secured by parachute troops.

Ground Forces visualised a glider that was to be a sort of flying pillbox, that would land before the main serials of transport gliders and parachute troops. This assault-glider would protect the landings against enemy infantry, small arms fire, and anti-aircraft fire. Two 50-calibre and two 30-calibre machine-guns mounted behind armour plate and manned by glidermen, plus two rocket-launchers, would give the glider substantial fire-power. Tow-planes for the attack glider were to be either bomber or fighter planes.

On 22 May 1943 the Materiel Command awarded contracts to Timm Aircraft Company and Christopher Company for an XAG-2 and an XAG-1 respectively. Each glider was to have a gross weight of 8,500lb and a towing speed of 240 miles per hour. Each was to be a low-wing cantilever monoplane, with place for six glidermen and a pilot and co-pilot. The gliders were to be of all-wood construction.

Christopher delivered a wind-tunnel model, but General B. W. Chidlaw criticized the glider as a 'dammed fool idea'. The assault-glider project was 'spiked' in September 1943.

Glider 'Snatch' Pick-up Technique

Numerous suggestions for using gliders came from the front as America gained combat experience. One idea was to land gliders on packed snow to resupply ground units in the arctic. Another was to land them on water, where suitable landing areas were not available. Still another idea was to use gliders in the routine supplying of weapons, ammunition, food and personnel to fixed and mobile ground and air-force units; it was pointed out that this method of supply would be especially useful for armoured operations. Another suggestion was to drop airborne maintenance repair-shops, housed in gliders, behind armoured units to maintain the armoured vehicles. It was also recommended that gliders should move airborne field hospitals from one location to another or evacuate wounded from combat areas.

At first many of these suggestions might have been far beyond the scope of the glider to accomplish, but they were made feasible by the

Pick-up hook folded to the fuselage of a Douglas C-47

Waco CG-4As ready for take-off. Note telephone wire attached to tow rope for pilot communication

development of a pick-up device. It enabled a flying tow-plane to whisk away a loaded glider from a standing position. In July 1943 Major Louis B. Magid Jr., on the staff of the Airborne Command at Fort Bragg, North Carolina, tested the device and its associated technique. In these tests a C-47 flying at 140 miles per hour snatched a glider off the ground with ease. Within seconds from the time the C-47's tow-hook seized the glider tow-rope slung between two upright poles, the glider was in the air and flying at 120 miles per hour. Major Magid reported that the engines of the aeroplane showed less strain during the pick-up than during a conventional take off. The technique was used with a fully-loaded glider with equally good results. Soon successful tests were being made in snatching gliders equipped with skids as take-off gear. Snatch-tests were conducted with the CG-13A and were successful.

This technique was soon being used in training, and after manoeuvres, to recover gliders. It saved dismantling thousands of gliders, which, without this new technique, would have had to be hauled out from constricted areas by truck. The snatch technique was also soon being used after combat operations to transport flyable gliders back to home bases. It was used to evacuate wounded in the European theatre and in Burma.

Double Tow

After tests held at Camp Mackall, North Carolina, in September 1943, it became commonplace for C-47's to tow two gliders in a staggered V formation. This double-tow arrangement had the advantage of decreasing the air space taken up by flights delivering airborne units into combat. This had additional benefits. It delivered troops in a more concentrated mass and doubled the towing capacity of the aeroplanes.

Parachutists also jumped from gliders in double tow. The results were more successful than had been expected, causing Colonel Ward S. Ryan, who had conducted the tests, to recommend that gliders be modified for the use of parachute troops. This was not done, however, as the AAF found that using gliders in this way would prove less efficient than using them to carry the regularly-constituted glider infantry and other glider-trained ground units.

Hamilcar 'Pick-a-Back'

During 1949 the AAF procured a British Hamilcar glider for test and evaluation. They also began studies to determine if the Hamilcar, or another glider, could be carried 'pick-a-back' (an aeroplane on top of a glider) as the Germans had done with the DFS-230. They used the P-38 fighter aeroplane attached to the top of the Hamilcar; although consideration was also given to using the P-38 with the CG-10A.

Preparing the 'clothes-line' for a glider snatch

Douglas C-47 'picking up' a Waco CG-4A in what became known as a glider 'snatch'

Pick-a-back glider delivery had several advantages over standard glider tow techniques. The combined aircraft was piloted en route to its objective by the pilot of the P-38. This would ease the problem of flying the glider hundreds of miles, sometimes with instruments alone as experienced in standard tow-rope flight. After releasing the glider, the P-38 would provide it with protection overhead against hostile air attacks. If the glider could be loaded with fuel for the combined aircraft, long-range flights could take place, enabling the shipment of gliders to distant theatres of war. This last point was important in view of the fact that glider operations overseas had had to be curtailed because there was inadequate shipping space for the enormous crates that gliders required.

However, there were serious disadvantages to the pick-a-back system. It was time-consuming to arrange the coupling of the two craft. Furthermore it meant that the much needed fighter would be grounded for unacceptable periods of time. Once airborne, in the event of a power failure in the P-38 (because the release mechanism was to be electrically operated) there would be difficulty in releasing the glider. It was foreseen that wing-loading differentials would make the combination difficult to fly. Although the study concluded that the idea was aerodynamically feasible, structurally and from the standpoint of weight and balance, nevertheless the disadvantages were too many, and the idea was allowed to die.

Tow-planes

In the spring of 1942 General Arnold directed the Materiel Command to determine the suitability of the various combat and transport aircraft as tugs for towing gliders. Wright Field conducted extensive tests from then until late in 1944. The results showed that the C-47, C-46, C-54, and C-60 transport aeroplanes, the A-25 attack-bomber, the B-25 bomber and the P-38 fighter, and any four-engined bomber or transport, were all suitable for towing the CG-4A and the CG-15A. If the P-38 was used, it would be necessary to place sand-bags in the nose of the glider.

The CG-13A could be towed by a C-46, a C-54, a B-17 or a B-24 in addition to the favoured C-47. However, by the end of 1944 tactical considerations as well as the performance and availability of the C-47 in all theatres of operation made it the outstanding tow-plane, most widely used.

SIX

Gliders of the Soviet Union

Strong evidence exists that the Soviet Union pioneered the development of a transport glider, and, in fact, produced the first such aircraft. Little known to the outside world, in 1923, only five years after the revolution, Soviet authorities began encouraging gliding. In that year the government sponsored the first all-union (all Soviet nations) gliding contest. The Moscow glider club had been organised several years earlier.

Through the 1920's Soviet interest focused chiefly on sports gliding. In the 1930s, however, the government decided to expand Soviet gliding activities. In 1931 a dramatic upsurge occurred when at the Ninth Party Congress held in January the Komsomol passed a resolution calling for an unheralded expansion of the gliding movement, announcing a threefold purpose for its resolution. Firstly, through a training programme it sought to build up an enormous pool of glider-pilots; secondly, through research and development, and testing of new glider models, it hoped to gain useful information for aeronautical research; thirdly, it was setting out to capture as many world records as it could.

The government built a glider factory in Moscow. It set a production goal of 900 primary trainers and 300 training gliders per year. It named Oleg K. Antonov, an aircraft engineer and designer, who was to become famous for his glider designs, to head the design and engineering effort at the plant.

Shortly after the Komsomol resolution had been passed, eighty leading glider and light plane designers assembled at Koktabel. They studied twenty-two glider designs, and selected seven for construction and for tests to be made in 1932. In retrospect the pace at which the whole movement progressed gives some indication of the importance the government placed on the programme.

In thirty-six days of tests Soviet glider pilots flew 662 flights, averaging more than an hour each, in the seven gliders to be tested and in other gliders from distant parts of the Soviet Union, establishing six new Russian records. During that year in a single flight V. A. Stepanchenok in a G-9 glider looped 115 times and flew upside-down for more than one minute. Soviet glider pilots went on to perform new and unexpected aerobatics, long distance tows and a multitude of other achievements. A feature at the meet was G. F. Groschev's 'TsK Komsala', a four-place glider designed for towed flight.

At the same meeting B. Borodin flew two passengers for more than four hours in a single flight and with this feat the transport glider was born. It was then up to some perceptive person to recognise the significance of the flight; and it appears that this was not long in coming. The idea of a multi-passenger, towed glider, as opposed to the two-passenger soaring glider already flown, must have blossomed in 1932 or 1933, as Groshev, designer of the transport glider GN-4, undoubtedly had a large, innovative glider on the drawing board in late 1932 or 1933 for in 1934 the Moscow glider factory produced this aircraft, the GN-4, a glider that could transport five passengers and was designed for towed flight.

By 1934 the Soviets could boast ten gliding schools, 230 gliding stations, and 57,000 trained glider pilots.

Around 1934 a new concept took hold, fostered by Lev Pavlovich Malinovskii, head of the Scientific Technical administration of the *Grazhdanskiy Vozdushniy Flot* (Civilian Air Fleet). Malinovskii conceived the idea of using a low-powered freight glider-plane, easy to produce and cheap to operate, to solve some of Russia's long-distance fast freight needs. The fully-laden glider would carry about a ton of goods and be powered by a single 100 h.p. engine. The engine would assist the tow-plane during take-off. Once safely airborne the glider would cast off and under its own power deliver its cargo to a distant terminus.

Because most of the models were underpowered, only one or two went beyond the experimental stage. Several apparently grew into sizeable 10-passenger models, and there is a strong likelihood that these models, with engines removed, became the first of the larger 20-passenger transport gliders developed and observed in Russia during the mid 1930s.

One of these the G-31, an 18-passenger glider, was built at the military institute in Leningrad. There are reports that the German fighter ace of World War I, General Ernst Udet, was in Moscow in 1935 and witnessed several giant gliders in tow in one of the Soviet celebrations in Moscow. Undoubtedly this experience prompted him to suggest the conversion of the promising flying observatory into a military transport glider (see German DFS 230 glider, p. 27).

A-7

The Antonov A-7, also known as the red-front (Rot-Front) RF-8, was one of the early Soviet military transport gliders. It won a design award for Oleg K. Antonov, the famous aeronautical engineer. The first models were built about the time World War II started (1939). In its high aspect-ratio, its 62.2-foot wing, and in its fuselage, it preserved many of the excellent flying characteristics of a sailplane. It was

37.7 feet long and carried eight equipped soldiers.

It had a retractable landing gear and all the latest instruments necessary to enable the pilot to handle the glider in all flyable weather; 400 were manufactured.

The Army used the A-7 extensively to support Soviet guerrillas operating against the Germans. The glider was towed by the IL-4, the SB-3 and the IL-2.

Technical Data

Glider Model: A-7
Type: assault glider
Crew: pilot
Dimensions
  Wing-span: 62.2ft
  Wing area: 335sq ft
  Fuselage
    Length: 37.7ft

Weight
  Cargo: 2,000lb
Loadings
  pilot, 8 equipped troops
Tow-planes
  Li-2, 5B-3

A-11 (G-11)

While some sources doubt that the A-11 was ever built, there is substantial evidence to prove its existence. The evidence shows that the A-11 was an improved version of the A-7 glider. It was similar in appearance to the A-7, except for the fact that it had a strut-braced wing.

Vladimir Gribovskii collaborated with Oleg K. Antonov in its design and development. It had a wing span of 82 feet and a length of 42 feet.

Reports also exist of a G-11 glider. In view of the fact that Gribovskii was the co-designer of the A-11, it is possible that the A-11 and the G-11 (Gribovskii-11) were one and the same glider, the A-11 at sometime taking the G-11 designation for unknown reasons.

Technical Data

Glider Model: A-11 (G-11)
Type: transport
Crew: pilot, co-pilot
Dimensions
  Wing-span: 82ft
Fuselage
  Length: 42ft

Weight
  Cargo: 4,400lb
Loadings
  pilot, co-pilot, 20 equipped troops

BDP (S-1)

In July 1941 the Bureau of Special Construction, OKB (*Osoboe Konstruktorskoe Buro*), ordered the production of a battle transport-glider BDP (*Boevoi Desantnyi Planer*). The first model was built within a month, and the first test-flight was made before the end of the summer.

The BDP (S-1), as it became, had a high cantilever wing 65.7 feet long, of wooden construction, with a high aspect ratio. It was tapered and had a wing-root dihedral. Trailing edge flaps were fitted.

The monocoque fuselage was oval shaped and accommodated a pilot and 20 fully-equipped troops. Gun-ports were built into the fuselage, from which glidermen could shoot at attacking aircraft or, while landing, at enemy troops. The wheel under-carriage was dropped after take-off and the glider landed on plywood runners.

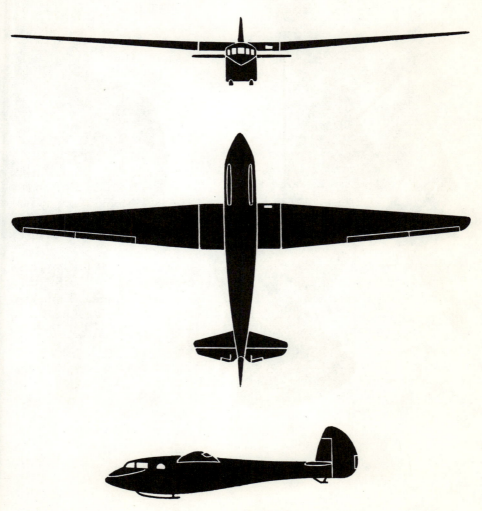

Antonov A-7, three-view section

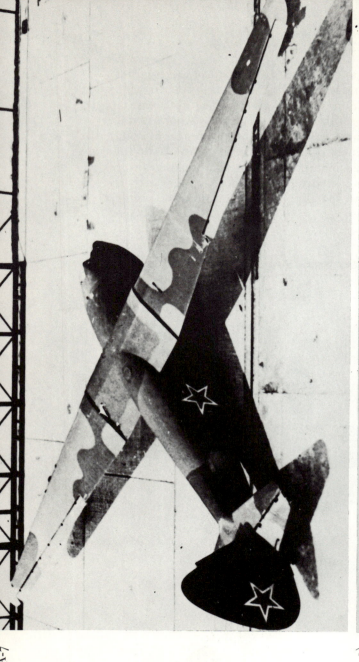

Antonov A-7

Polikarpov BDP (s-1)

The government stopped production shortly after the first gliders were manufactured, deploying the factory to the east in Russia to escape destruction by the advancing Nazi armies. Production of the BDP (S-1) was not resumed because the government turned all aircraft production resources toward the construction of combat aircraft.

Technical Data

Glider Model(s): BDP(S-1)
Type: battle glider
Crew: pilot
Dimensions
   Wing-span: 65.7ft
   Wing area: 481sq ft
Weight
   Total with cargo: 7,700lb
   Empty: 5,070lb
   Cargo: 2,630lb

Loadings
   20 soldiers, equipped, or equivalent weight in other cargo.
Flight performance
   Maximum airspeed: 100mph

Motor-Glider MP-I

The motor-glider MP-1 (*motoplaner*-1) showed the wartime continuation of Russian hopes to develop a satisfactory powered glider—long a dream of glider advocates. This development took place in 1943 just before the deployment of the factory to the east. The MP and the BDP (S-1) differed only in minor detail, except for the installation of two 140 h.p. five-cylinder engines on the leading edge of the wing of a standard BDP (S-1). A fixed-wheel landing gear was installed, also hoops at the ends of the wings to protect the tips on landing. A trim-tab was fitted to the rudder, and a small window at the bottom of the nose to give the pilot better visibility.

The MP-1 had to be assisted at take-off when carrying a full load, but when empty could take off without assistance. It was released by its tow-plane once airborne and flew at 100 miles per hour, having a range of close to 500 miles.

Glider-Bomber PB

During 1942 the OKB considered building a single-seat glider-bomber, the PB (*Planer Bombardirovshchik*) and produced plans for it. These called for the glider to have an internal bomb bay that would allow for a variety of loads, including supply containers and a 4,400lb bomb. The project was dropped, however, perhaps because of the urgent need for facilities and materials to build combat aircraft.

G-31

The G-31 military glider was a daring experiment far ahead of its time. It was designed by Pavel Ignat'evich Grokhovskii, military pilot, parachutist, and inventor, and head of the special design bureau of the Leningrad Institute.

It was a mid-wing all-wooden monoplane. The fuselage was a narrow plywood monocoque construction that used wood-fabrication techniques advanced for that day. The pilot and co-pilot sat above the wing in a plexiglass enclosure. The forward edge of the wing, which was 91.9 feet long, was transparent for approximately sixteen feet on each side of the fuselage. Eighteen passengers, nine on each side, lay flat in the wing behind the transparent window.

The G-31 gliderplane or powered glider, *Yakov Alksnis*, followed the development of the G-31 glider. A 700 h.p. M-25 9-cylinder radial engine, placed in the nose, powered the Yakov Alksnis.

After flight tests of these gliders had been conducted at Moscow, it became clear that the design did not allow for quick enough abandonment of the glider by its passengers in an emergency or when landing under fire in combat. For this reason the G-31 and G-31 Yakov Alksnis were abandoned.

Technical Data

Glider Model: G-31
Type: transport glider
Crew: pilot, co-pilot
Dimensions
    Wing-span: 91.9ft
    Wing area: 753sq ft
Weight
    Total with cargo: 7,054lb
    Empty: 3,086lb
    Cargo: 3,968lb

Loadings
    18 troops, equipped.
Flight performance
    Maximum airspeed:
    84mph

GN-4

The GN-4 (*Groshev* No. 4) designed by G. F. Groshev, was built at the Moscow Glider Factory shortly after the factory's establishment. It was first revealed to the public in the 1934 all-union glider meeting.

This was the world's first transport glider. In design it stood between the sailplane and the wartime transport glider, although in configuration it was much like a large sailplane. Although designed to be towed throughout its flight, except for the few minutes after its release from its tow-plane, it is reputed to have flown as a sailplane under suitable wind conditions. It was primarily designed for flying as one of a combination of gliders in a glider train, and was normally towed by the commercial version of the R-5.

The GN-4 was a strut-braced high-wing monoplane with a narrow oval fuselage. It had an enclosed pilot's compartment with five passenger seats behind the pilot. The 60-foot wing had a straight

Groshev GN-4, the world's first military transport glider

leading edge and a trailing edge tapered from the centre section. It had a very high aspect ratio. The R-5 towed it at close to 100 miles per hour. The empty weight of the glider was 1,000 pounds.

Technical Data

Glider Model(s): GN-4	*Weight*
Type: transport glider	Total with cargo: 1,992lb
Crew: pilot	Empty: 1,000lb
Dimensions	Cargo: 992lb
Wing-span: 60ft	*Loadings*
Fuselage	5 passengers
Length: 27ft	*Flight performance*
	Towing speed: 100mph

IL-32

The IL-32 was designed by S. V. Ilyushin and a single glider, a prototype, was finished in 1948. No others were built.

It was an all-metal, high-wing, cantilever monoplane. A unique feature was that both the nose and the rear of the cargo compartment were hinged to permit the loading of heavy or bulky equipment. The glider had built-in ramps for loading wheeled cargo.

It carried a crew and thirty-five fully-equipped soldiers.

Technical Data

Glider Model: IL-32	*Loadings*
Type: heavy-transport glider	35 soldiers, equipped
Crew: pilot, co-pilot	

KT-20

Conceived in 1944 by D. N. Kolesnikov and P. V. Tsybin, well-known in the Soviet Union as pioneers in glider design, the KT-20 (named after the designers) was a large transport glider. A few were built in

Ilyushin Il-32

the Yakovlov factory. It had a sharply-tapered strut-braced wing 72.6 feet long and a tapered fuselage 49.4 feet long.

The KT-20 was loaded from the rear. The section beyond the trailing edge of the wing lifted upward to open the cargo compartment. It was constructed of wood and metal and carried twenty-four troops or 4,410 pounds of cargo. It was towed by the IL-12.

Technical Data
Glider Model: KT-20
Type: transport glider
Crew: pilot, co-pilot
Dimensions
    Wing-span: 72.6ft
    Fuselage
    Length: 49ft

Weight
    Cargo: 4,410lb
Tow-plane: IL-12

SAM-23

In 1943, in addition to the KC-20 and the BDP (S-1), the Soviets produced the SAM-23. It was a high-wing, twin-boom, sturdily-built monoplane resembling the U.S. YCG-10A. A. S. Moskalev, its

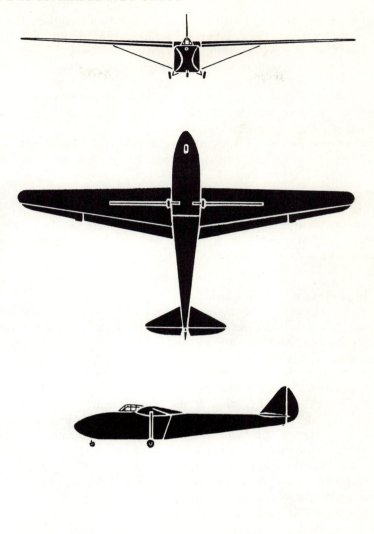

Tsybin KT-20, three-view section and Moskalev SAM-23

designer, conceived a 'gondola' fuselage, and so designed the SAM that it efficiently loaded and carried bulky cargo, including Jeep-sized vehicles. The pilot and co-pilot sat in the nose behind a large concave plexiglass window which allowed excellent observation.

The glider had an integral ramp that was lowered when the rear of the cargo compartment was raised, and was propped up between the booms for loading. It could carry sixteen men or a Jeep, or an equivalent weight in other cargo.

The Soviets produced a number of SAM-23's. Moskalev also proposed a motorised SAM, but the project never developed beyond the design stage.

Technical Data

Glider Model: SAM-23	*Loadings*
Type: battle transport glider	16 equipped troops or a
Crew: pilot, co-pilot	Jeep or the equivalent of
Weight	other cargo.
Cargo: 3,600lb	

Jakovleva-Cybina Glider

This glider was reportedly shown at the Moscow Soviet Aviation Day exhibitions in 1949. Six were designed and built under the direction of A. S. Jakovleva, and another six under the direction of aeronautical engineer P. V. Cybina.

It is possibly the same craft as the medium-sized Tshibin cargo-glider, since the likelihood of two new gliders appearing at this date is questionable. On the other hand, descriptions of the Jakovleva-Cybina, and the fact that there appears to be no question that one glider was designed and built by these two engineers and the other by Tshibin (in his own right a prominent aircraft designer), lead to the conclusion that there were, in fact, two new and different models. It is interesting that descriptions of the Jakovleva-Cybina glider and the American World War II CG-4 are similar; and it is quite evident that the Jakovleva-Cybina and the CG-4 are alike in appearance.

The Jakovleva-Cybina glider had a large 'greenhouse', giving the pilot and co-pilot excellent visibility relatively free from interference from structural bracing. It carried troops or cargo, and could be used for parachute drops. It was fabric covered, and opened from the front for loading. The towing aeroplane was the Il-12.

Winged Tank 'KT'

Around 1941 it was rumoured in Soviet circles that the Soviet Army was in the process of developing a glider transport system that could carry a small battle-tank. Reports about this project more recently available, tend to confirm the fact that such a project did exist.

Assisted by a staff of engineers, Oleg K. Antonov was charged with the development and construction of what came to be known as the transport glider KT (*Kryliatyi Tank* or Winged Tank). The project apparently started in 1939 or 1940 and was completed in 1941, when the system was tested.

The KT was a new departure in transport glider design in several major respects. One very interesting feature is that it was a biplane glider. Secondly, Antonov used the T-60 tank as the fuselage of the glider; this combination could be towed into the air and released while in flight to glide down to a pre-selected spot behind enemy lines. The T-60 six-ton tank, its gun pointing to the rear, was secured between the twin booms of the glider and attached to the under surface of the lower wing. A substantial part of the tank protruded ahead of the lead edge of the lower wing. The system was so designed that the controls for the glider were inside the tank.

In view of the shortage of metal in the Soviet Union at the time, the glider frame was made of wood, and the wings and empennage were covered with fabric.

With the test pilot Sergei Anokin at the controls of the winged tank, Pasha Jeremejew, at the controls of a four-engined TB-3 bomber, towed the enormous weight into the air. Although the take-off and early stages of the flight went well, the bomber's engines began to overheat, and the glider had to be released. Anokin started the tank's engine, and then let the tank treads start to move slowly. At about 200 feet above the ground he accelerated the treads; they reached their maximum land speed just before the treads touched the ground. The system landed smoothly, and Anokin brought it to a stop. The tank was quickly disengaged from its wings, and it raced off.

Despite the success of the first flight, no others took place, reportedly because there was a shortage of towing aeroplanes with enough power to tow the winged tank, such planes then being urgently needed at the front.

Technical Data

Glider Model: Winged tank
  KT
Type: battle-tank transport
  glider
Dimensions
  Wing-span: 49.2ft
  Wing area: 732sq ft
  Fuselage
  Length: 37.7ft

Weight
  Total with cargo: 18,000lb
  Empty: 4,800lb
  Cargo: 13,200lb
Loadings
  1 six-ton, T-60 tank
Flight performance
  Lift off speed: 100mph
Tow-plane: TB-3 bomber

Ts-25

First seen by the public in 1948 at the Soviet Aviation Day exhibition in Moscow, the Ts-25 was one of the largest of the post-war Soviet gliders to go into production. At the time of the exhibition, six had been manufactured. It had many of the design characteristics of the wartime KT-20, for which Tsybin was a co-designer, and in one way can be considered a technologically sophisticated successor to the KT-20.

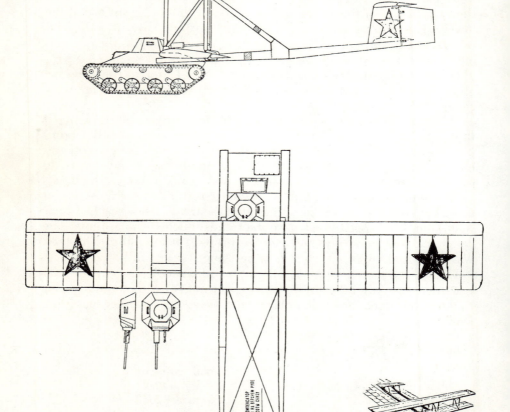

Antonov Kryliatyi tank KT 'winged tank', three-view section

Designed by P. V. Tsybin, the Ts-25 was a heavy cargo-glider. It had a braced high wing and a pilot's compartment sitting above the cargo compartment. The nose was hinged to facilitate loading. The wheels could be dropped, after which the pilot landed the glider on skids fitted to the bottom of the craft. The glider appeared to be constructed largely of wood, with wing and fuselage exteriors of stressed plywood.

The Soviets furnished a number of the Ts-25's to the Czechoslovak military forces, who called it the NK 25.

Technical Data

Glider Model: Ts-25
Type: cargo glider
Crew: pilot, co-pilot
Dimensions
  Wing-span: 82.8ft
  Wing area: 830sq ft
  Fuselage
    Length: 54.1ft
Weight
  Total with cargo: 9,921lb
  Empty: 5,115lb
  Cargo: 4,806lb

Loadings
  25 troops, equipped, small vehicles, light artillery, or miscellaneous cargo.
Flight performance
  Maximum airspeed: 155mph

YAK-14

The Yak-14, a large, bulky, square-shaped wooden glider was designed by A. S. Yakovlev and produced shortly after the war. This glider and the Ts-25 caused a sensation at the Soviet Aviation Day Show held at the Tushino Airport near Moscow in 1949, when six of each flew overhead in what was described as 'spectacular glider-trains'.

The Yak-14 had a high-aspect-ratio braced wing with a span of 85.8 feet. The wing was built from three sections, a rectangular centre section and two tapered outer sections that were square at the ends. The wing had no dihedral. Fowler flaps and slotted ailerons extended over the whole of the trailing edge.

The nose opened sideways to permit the loading of cargo. The pilot and co-pilot sat in the nose, which featured a large 'greenhouse', giving the pilot excellent visibility relatively unobstructed by structural bracing.

The Yak-14 carried small vehicles or other cargo to the extent of 7,716lb, or could transport thirty-five fully-equipped soldiers, and it could be used to drop parachutists. The cargo compartment measured 26.3 feet in length by 7.6 feet in height and was 7.4 feet wide. The maximum towing speed was 186 miles per hour.

Tsybin TS-25

Yakovlev Yak-14

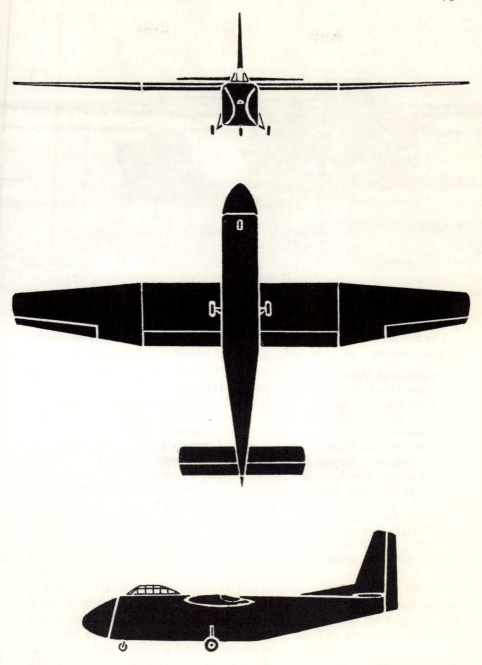

Yakovlev Yak-14

In mid 1943, under a subsequent contract calling for a somewhat modified version with a wing-span of 50.5 feet and slightly larger fuselage, de Havilland built six DHA-G2's (RAAF's A57-1/6's). The empty weight was 1,450 pounds and the glider carried 1,800 pounds.

With the exception of one DHA-G2, which after the war was converted to a Griffith suction-wing test-glider using a contrifugal fan driven by a Mercury 59A, 96hp engine, the gliders had an indifferent

De Havilland DHA-G1, three-view section

career. They were used in limited operations with the School of Land/
Air Warfare.

Technical Data

Glider Model(s) : DHA-G1,
    DHA-G2
Type: transport glider
Crew: pilot
Dimensions
    Wing-span: 59ft, 50.5ft
    Wing area: 300sq ft
    Fuselage
      Length: 33ft, 33ft
      Height: 7ft, 7ft

Weight
    Total with cargo:
      2,790lb, 3,250lb
    Empty:
      1,240lb, 1,450lb
    Cargo:
      1,550lb, 1,800lb
Loadings
    Six troops, equipped.
Flight performance
    Maximum towing speed:
    130mph
    Maximum airspeed:
    200mph

Canada

In 1942 the Royal Canadian Air Force contemplated purchasing
thirty Hotspur gliders from the United Kingdom to use in training a
cadre of Canadian glider pilots in a school then being considered by
the Air staff. Thought was also given to organizing a glider operational
training unit. None of these plans materialized, however.

Later that year, apparently modifying its plans, the Air Force did
purchase twenty-two Hotspur IIs, and presumably many Canadians
did learn to fly them. Canadians piloted gliders in some of the most
important glider operations in Europe. In one of the most daring
glider flights in history, with one Canadian and one RAF pilot at the
controls, a CG-4A carrying medical supplies and other critical items
was towed across the Atlantic Ocean from Canada to England.

After the war the RAF obtained three Horsas, thirty-two Hadrian
Mark IIs (CG-4As), a CG-15A and one PG-2A. RAF inventories
carried these gliders for as long as ten years after the war.

China

Shortly after World War II the Nationalist Chinese Air Force ordered
the production of an assault glider. The Institute of Aero Research at
Chengtu in Szechwan Province completed the first prototype in 1947.
It carried a pilot, co-pilot and twelve passengers. It was one of the few
low-wing transport gliders built during or after the war, possessing a
surprisingly streamlined appearance. It was of wood construction,
doped with aluminum. Although twelve were ultimately produced,
the glider remained experimental, and there were no production
orders placed.

De Havilland DHA-G1

Glas II Suction Wing glider (a converted de Havilland DHA-G2)

Chinese glider

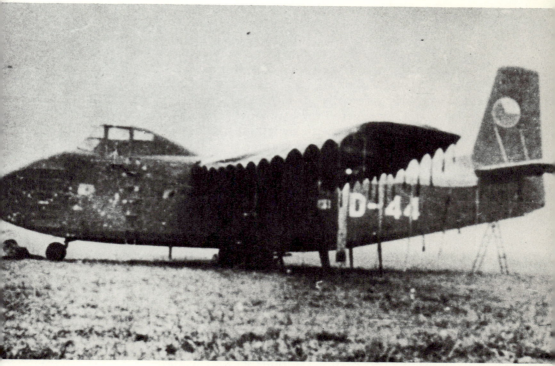

NK-14, Czechoslovakia (Soviet Yak-14)

Czechoslovakia

Gliding and soaring long have been popular sports in Czechoslovakia. Although during the war, while dominated by the Nazis, little took place in glider development, after the war, particularly in the late 1940s that country's armed forces took a serious interest in transport gliders. By the early 1950s the country had two under construction, the AE-53 and the LD-605.

The AE-53 had much the appearance of the American Laister-Kaufmann YCG-10A, the LD-605 resembled the CG-4A. Each had comparable loading ports to their American counterparts. Before the two had reached completion, the Soviets turned over numbers of the Ts-25s and YAK-14s to the Czechoslovakian Air Force, and the construction of the AE-53 and LD-605 was discontinued.

France: Castel-Mauboussin CM 10

After the invasion of France by the Allies and the recapture of Paris, the soon-reorganised French Air Ministry determined to investigate the possibility of using the transport glider for military operations. French military leaders had been impressed by the Allied assault-glider operations in various phases of the war against Germany.

The Ministry requested the *Établissement Fouga*, headed by Mr Pierre Mauboussin (a company that specialized in designing and building sports gliders) to design and build a military glider similar to those used by the Royal Air Force and the U.S. Air Force. The glider initially took the name *Castel Mauboussin*, 'Castel' being derived from 'Castello', the originally Spanish name of Robert Castello, the technical design manager of the company. It was he who had proposed a high-wing monoplane with a high lift-to-drag ratio.

The Ministry ordered two prototypes. The first was delivered in 1947 (although its design and construction had begun before the end of the war). Despite the fact that the French had just been liberated from German occupation, and the economy was weak and materials in short supply, the glider turned out to be a superb aircraft.

Aerodynamically the *Mauboussin* was a clean aircraft of all-wood construction. It had a wing-span of 87 feet and a length of 60 feet. It loaded from the front, the nose swinging open at the side to permit loading to take place. It could carry two $\frac{1}{4}$-ton trucks, or a $\frac{1}{4}$-ton truck and a howitzer with trailer as well as gun crew and driver.

The first test-flight took place at Mont-de-Marson with test-pilot Leon Bourriau at the controls. The flight was successful, as was the programme of evaluation-testing, until the final phases when Bourriau unknowingly exceeded stress limits set for the glider. The CM 10 disintegrated, and although Bourriau managed to eject and came to the

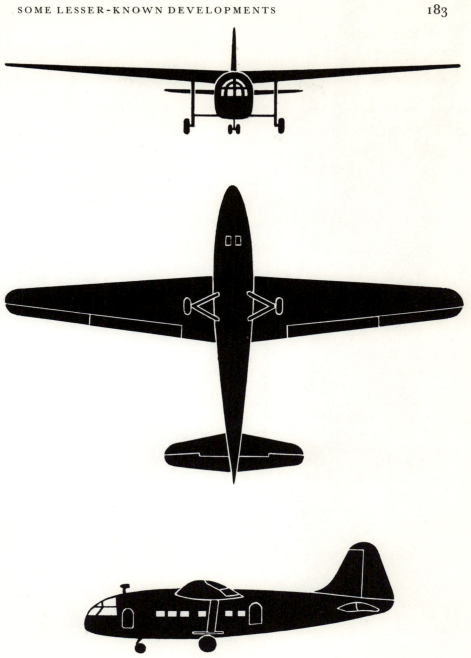

Castel Mauboussin CM 10, three-view section

Castel Mauboussin
CM 10

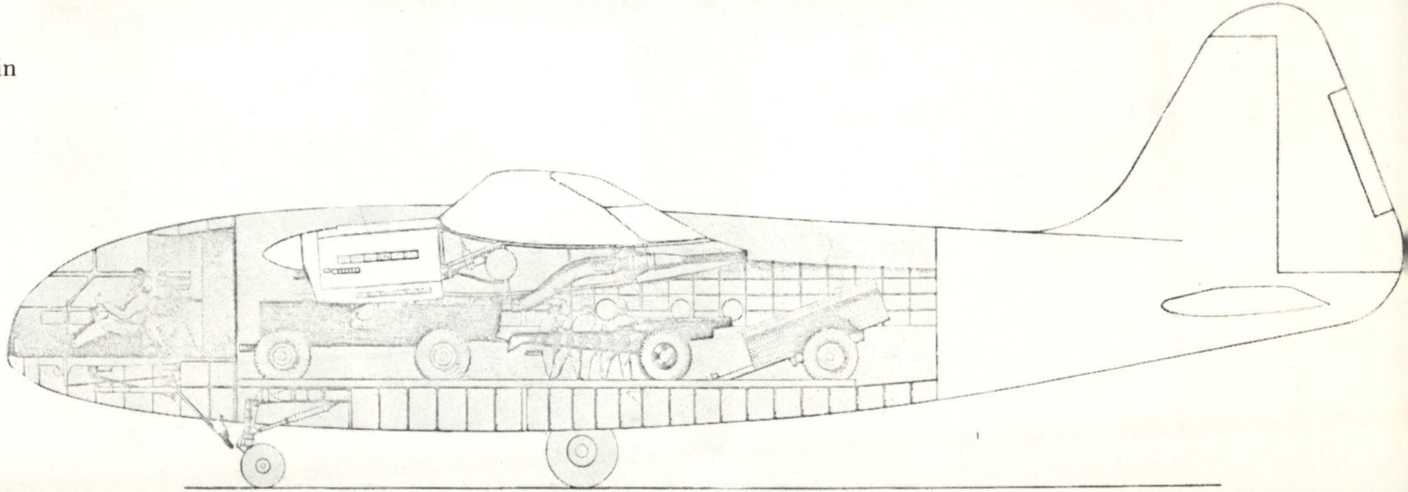

Castel Mauboussin
CM 10, exploded
drawing

ground by parachute he was severely injured.

The glider, nevertheless, was considered an unquestionable success, and before testing was completed the Ministry placed a pre-production order for twenty-five gliders with the Société National de Construction Aeronautiques du Nord. Later the number was increased to a hundred. The Société National had been called in because the Fouga facilities were inadequate to meet the production requirements. Before production had really got under way, however, budget changes made it necessary to cut production, and only six were ever manufactured.

Several production models were later converted into powered aircraft. One was fitted with two piston engines, another with jets. However, neither project succeeded, despite its attractive performance as a glider, and later in its powered 100 and 101 versions. The demise of the CM 10 was the result of the change of French military thinking, which gave priority to paratroops over glider-borne forces. In addition, there was a surplus of powered aircraft in France after the war, including the Ju 2 and the C-47. Budgetary cutbacks also played an important role in reducing the chance of the CM 10 taking a solid place in the military and civilian aviation industry.

Technical Data

Glider Model: CM10 (Castel-Mauboussin)
Type: Heavy transport glider
Crew: pilot, co-pilot
Dimensions
  Wing-span: 87ft
  Wing area: 770sq ft
  Fuselage
    Length: 60ft
    Height: 19ft
  Cargo compartment
    Length: 26ft
    Width: 5.8ft
    Height: 7ft

Weight
  Total with cargo: 15,400lb
  Empty: 6,400lb
  Cargo: 9,000lb
Loadings
  35 troops, equipped; two $\frac{1}{4}$-ton trucks; or military equipment to load capacity
Flight performance
  Tow speed: 180mph
Tow-planes: Ju 52, Halifax, SO 161, C-47

India

Strangely, India in 1941 and 1942 was one of the first nations to produce a military transport glider, even though the centres of World War II conflict were still fairly removed from her borders. It was not until early 1944 that General Orde Wingate launched Imperial glider forces against the Japanese in Burma in the most innovative airborne campaign of the war. U.S. gliders piloted by Americans transported these troops on more than ten glider missions of that campaign.

Hindustan Aircraft G 1

Ambrosini AL 12P

Anticipating extensive airborne operations in the Eastern theatre, Britain negotiated to build 40 Horsas in India, but a contract was never signed. Lawrence Wright in *The Wooden Sword* points out high costs as the major factor, since bids showed it would cost ten times as much to produce the Horsa there as it was then costing in England.

The British shipped some Horsas to India, but the idea of sending quantities was shelved, since four-engine tow-planes necessary for towing the heavy glider in the tepid climate and to the heights necessary to cross mountain ranges on future missions were not available in quantity in India.

Lawrence Wright also reports the Indians did use and apparently took over some CG-4As for training their own glider pilots.

G-1

Engineers Dr V. M. Ghatage, F. M. Crane and M. C. McCarthy, Jr., of Hindustan Aircraft Limited designed the G-1 transport glider during 1941 and 1942. It was a semi-monocoque wood glider that carried eight passengers, a pilot and a co-pilot. A two-ply moulded plywood with wood grain at 45° to the longitudinal axis of the glider covered the fuselage.

The cockpit enclosure was of moulded, framed, transparent plastic panels, designed to give the pilots excellent visibility. It could be raised to allow pilot entrance and in case of emergency could be jettisoned to permit rapid escape. It had a large passenger door on the right side just back of the last passenger seat.

Plywood covered the built-up truss ribs of the 56.7-foot single-spar wing. The wing had spoilers on the upper surface near the leading edge midway in the semi-span. The rudder and elevators were covered with fabric.

The glider had dual controls, and pilots sat in tandem. It had jettisonable wheels and a single hard wood ski.

Technical Data

Glider Model: G-1
Type: assault/transport glider
Crew: pilot, co-pilot
Dimensions
    Wing-span: 56.7ft
    Wing area: 300sq ft
    Fuselage
      Length: 30.5ft
      Height: 11.1ft

Weight
    Total with cargo: 4,000lb
    Empty: 1,500lb
    Cargo: 2,500lb
Loadings
    8 passengers
    or cargo.
Flight performance
    Maximum airspeed:
    160mph
    Aspect ratio: 10

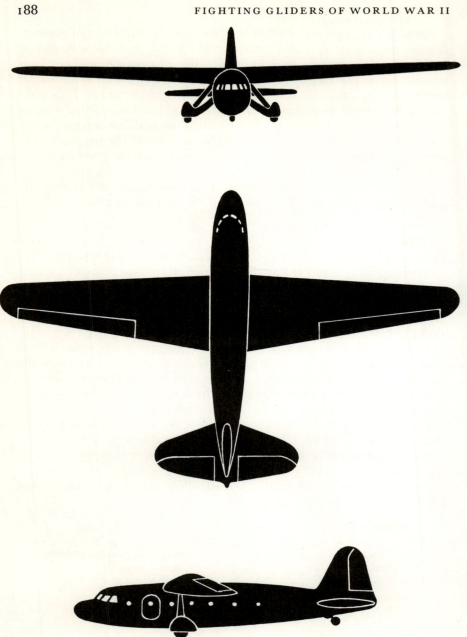

Ambrosini Al 12P, three-view section

Unique among allied gliders and in keeping with German glider doctrine that the glider should be a fighting weapon as opposed to just a passive transport vehicle, plastic windows had gun ports through which occupants could fire their rifles while in flight. The G-1 weighed 4,000 pounds and could carry 2,500. Hindustan Aircraft produced a single prototype and parts for ten more. Lawrence Wright in *The Wooden Sword* reports wing warpage on the prototype, a probable reason that the ten were never assembled, and the glider never went into production.

Italy

Italy formed its first glider transport organization in June 1942. Initially the Italians flew the German Go 242 and the DFS 230. As the war progressed, the military leaders determined to build their own gliders, and several models were ultimately produced.

Italian gliders and glider pilots were marshalled for the Malta operation as part of the total of a more than 500 glider operation planned by the Axis.

AL-12P

The Ambrosini AL-12P was built in 1942 by the Aerolombardi Corporation at the 'Cantu' (Como Province) works. Its designer was A. Ambrosini, and its project engineer Ermengildo Preti.

A cantilever high-wing monoplane glider designed for attack and transport purposes, its tubular, 47-foot-long, wood-ribbed fuselage was covered with stressed moulded plywood secured to the ribs. The 70-foot wing had a 'double-box' foliated spruce plywood spar; plywood covered the wing surface, although ailerons were fabric-covered. Large slotted spoilers could be activated to stand perpendicularly above and below the wing, and were one of the advanced features of this very well-designed glider.

Technical Data

Glider Model: AL-12P
Type: attack and transport
  glider
Crew: pilot, co-pilot
Dimensions
  Wing-span: 70ft
  Wing area: 630sq ft
  Fuselage
   Length: 47ft
  Cargo compartment
   Length: 22ft
   Width: 5.8ft

Weight
  Total with cargo: 6,200lb
  Empty: 3,500lb
  Cargo: 2,700lb
Loadings
  12 equipped troops or
  equivalent weight

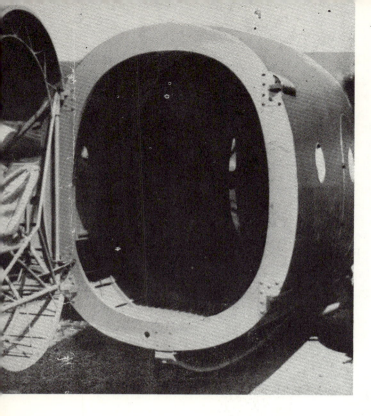

Ambrosini AL 12P

Spoilers of Ambrosini AL 12P

The nose of welded steel tubing was covered with plywood into which large plexiglass windows were set. Pilots sat side by side in the nose, which was hinged on the right side to open for the loading of cargo. There was a side door from which paratroopers jumped. The fuselage had seven equally-spaced windows on each side. The empennage was plywood-covered.

The glider carried twelve fully-equipped troops, or 2,700lb of other weight. It was test-flown in 1943 and proved to be an excellent glider. Aerolombardi produced sixteen of these gliders for the Italian Army, and some were used in operations fitted with 195 horse-power Alfa-115, four cylinder, aircooled engines, it became the P-512.

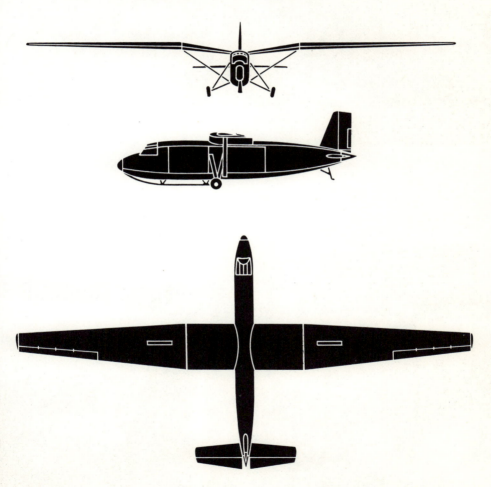

Caproni TM 2, three-view section

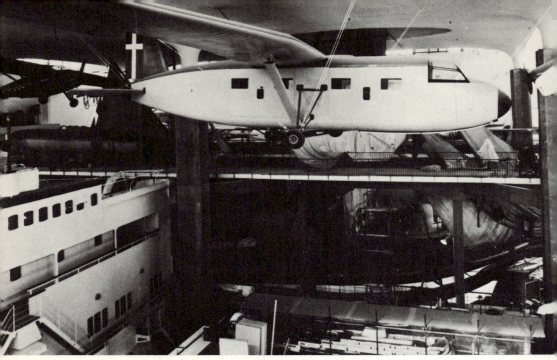

Caproni TM 2

AB Flygindustri Fi 3

TM-2 (CATTM-2)

Designed by Caproni's Ing. Del Proposto, the TM-2 (CATTM-2) made its first flight in 1943. It was a large glider that had a loaded weight of 8,800 pounds and carried twenty passengers.

It was all-wood construction with plywood and fabric covering. Four large doors opened into the cargo compartment, facilitating loading. It had a wing span of 74.8 feet and was 42.5 feet long.

In one of the early test flights the TM-2 went into a spin, killing the pilot. The glider was still not accepted for production at the time of the armistice.

The Caproni Corporation planned to equip the glider with motors but did not go through with the idea. The prototype, one of the few World War II gliders still in existence, is in the Milan Museum.

Technical Data

Glider Model: TM-2
  (CATTM-2)
Type: transport glider
Crew: pilot, co-pilot
Dimensions
  Wing-span: 74.8ft
  Wing area: 495sq ft
  Fuselage:
    Length: 42.5ft
    Height: 15.5ft
  Cargo compartment
    Length: 23.4ft
    Width: 4ft
    Height: 8ft

Weight
  Total with cargo: 8,800lb
  Empty: 4,400lb
  Cargo: 4,400lb
Loadings
  20 equipped troops or equivalent weight in cargo

Sweden: FI-3

The A B Flygindustri, Halmst ad, Sweden, received a requirement from the Swedish Air Force for a transport glider in 1941. From this period until the end of World War II the company produced five FI-3 gliders.

Technical Data

Glider Model: FI-3
Type: transport glider
Crew:
Dimensions
  Wing-span: 54.6ft
  Wing area: 344.5sq ft
  Fuselage
    Length: 30.8ft

Weight
  Total with cargo: 3,970lb
  Empty: 1,742lb
  Cargo: 2,228lb
Loadings
  II troops, equipped

They were of wooden construction and had fabric covering. Doors were quickly detachable panels on each side of the fuselage.

The FI-3 had a wing span of 54.6 feet and a length of 30.8 feet. Fully loaded the glider weighed 3,970 pounds.

At the end of World War II the Swedish Air Force terminated the programme.

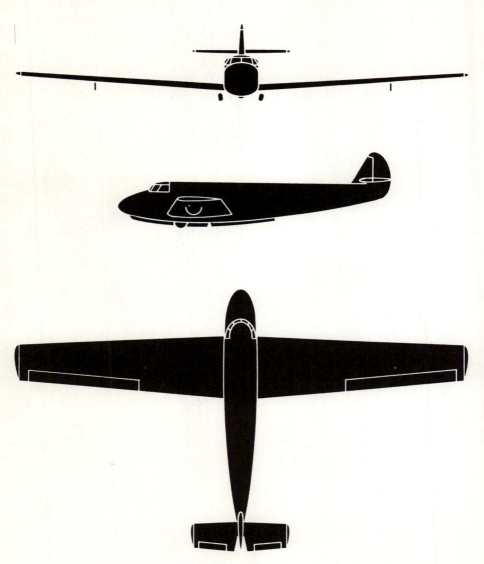

Turkish Air League THK 1, three-view section

Turkish Air League THK I

Ivo Sostaric glider

Turkey: THK-1

In 1941, alert to new developments in aviation, the Turkish Air Force decided to examine the potentialities of the transport glider. It issued a requirement for a transport glider to the Türk Hava Kurumu (Turkish Air League) THK.

By 1943 the League had produced the THK-1, an all-wood glider that carried a pilot and eleven passengers.

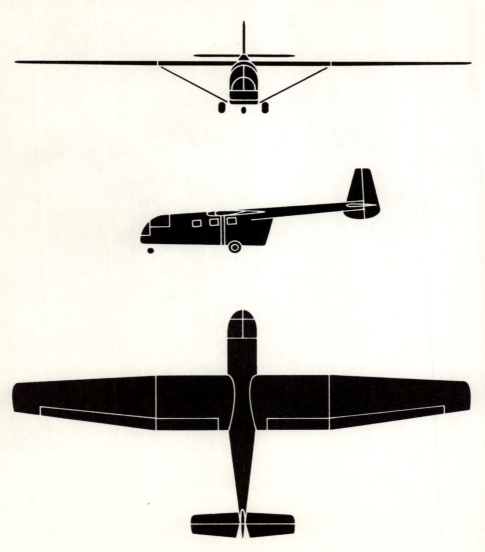

Ivo Sostaric glider, three-view section

Although some tests were conducted, the Turkish Air Force lost interest in the project, and the development of the glider was terminated.

Yugoslavia

After World War II Yugoslavia decided to investigate the possibilities of the transport glider as a military weapon that would fit into her armament requirements. It carried a single small vehicle or twelve passengers in a pod-like fuselage that opened at the rear to enable loading of bulky equipment. Its high braced wing was set well back over the fuselage. It had a single boom and a fixed tricycle landing gear. Only one such glider was built. It was designed by Ivo Sostarie.

APPENDIX I ———————————

Glider Data

	Span (feet)	Wing Area (sq. ft.)	Empty	Cargo	Total	Troops*	Built
			Weights				
Argentina							
I.AE.25	83.7	851.42	5,423	2,474	7,897	13	1
Australia							
DHA-G1	59	300	1,240	1,550	2,790	6	2
(EG-1, 2)							
DHA-G2	50.5		1,450	1,800	3,250	6	6
(A57-1/6)							
Canada							
Horsa	88	1,204	8,370	7,130	15,750	25	3
Hotspur I	62				3,600	8	22
Hadrian Mark II	84	852	3,440	4,060	7,500	13	32
(U.S. CG-4A)							
CG-15A	62.1	623	4,000	4,000	8,000	13	1
(U.S. CG-15)							
China							
No designation				2,800		12	12
Czechoslovakia							
NK-25	same as data on Ts-25 (see *Soviet Union*)						
Yak-14	(see *Soviet Union*)						
France							
CM-10	87	770	6,400	9,000	15,400	35	6
Germany							
Assault/transport							
DFS 230	72	444	1,800	2,800	4,600	9	2,230
DFS 230 V7	63	425	3,520	4,180	7,700	15	1
Go 242	79	690	7,000	8,000	15,000	23	1,528
Me 321	181	3,230	26,000	44,000	70,000	200	200
Ju 322	203	6,400	56,000	24,000	90,000		2
DFS 331	71	646	4,500	5,500	10,000	18	1
Go 345A	67	537	5,450	3,500	8,950	12	2
Assault							
Ka 430	64	435	3,750	3,750	7,500	12	12
Fighter							
BV 40	26	94	1,844	250	2,094	1	19
India							
G-1	56.7	300	1,500	2,500	4,000	8	1
Italy							
AL-12P	70	630	3,500	2,700	6,200	12	16
TM-2	74.8	495	4,400	4,400	8,800	20	1
Japan							
Army							
Ku-1	55	324	1,540	1,320	2,860	6–8	100

	Wing		Weights			Troops*	Built
	Span (feet)	Area (sq. ft)	Empty	Cargo	Total		
Ku-6	72.3	649	1,538	6,174	7,712		1
Ku-7	114	1,288	10,000	16,455	26,455	32	9
Ku-8	76	544	3,750	3,950	7,700	18	700
Ku-11	60	475	2,800	2,600	5,400	12	3
Navy							
MXY5	59.4	475	3,520	2,240	5,940	11	12
Soviet Union							
A-7	62.2	335		2,000		8	400
BDP (S-1)	65.7	485	5,070	2,630	7,700	20	7
A-11, (G-11)	82	440		4,400		20	1
G-31	91.9	753	3,086	3,968	7,054	18	1
GN-4	60		1,000	992	1,992	5	1
IL-32				8,000		35	1
KT-20	72.6	840		4,410		24	2
SAM-23				3,600		16	1
Tank-delivery							
(Winged Tank)	49.2	732	4,800	13,200	18.000		1
Ts-25	82.8	830	5,115	4,806	9,921	25	6
Yak-14	85.8	1,050	6,800	7,716	14,900	35	413
Sweden							
FI-3	54.6	344.5	1,742	2,228	3,970	11	5
Turkey							
THK-1				2,400		11	1
United Kingdom							
Hadrian	84	852	3,444	4,060	7,500	13	746
(U.S. CG-4A)							
Hamilcar (half scale prototype)							1
Hamilcar	110	1,657	18,000	17,500	36,000	40	412
Hengist	80	780	4,666	3,667	8,333	15	18
Horsa I	88	1,104	8,370	7,130	15,500	25	2,302
Horsa II	88	1,104	8,370	7,380	15,750	28	1,490
Hotspur I	62				3,600	7	18
Hotspur II	45.9	272	1,755	1,880	3,635	7	997
Hotspur III	45.9	272	1,660	1,940	3,600	7	50
Hotspur twin	58	262	3,025	3,525	6,550	14	1
United States							
Army Air Force							
XCG-1						7	0
XCG-2						13	0
CG-3A	73	420	2,400	2,400	4,400	7	100
XCG-4	83.6	852	3,440	4,066	7,500	13	1
CG-4A	83.6	852	3,440	4,060	7,500	13	13,909
XCG-4B	83.6	852				13	1
XCG-5						7	1
XCG-6							0
XCG-7	80	600	5,000	2,000	7,000	7	1
XCG-8	90	880	7,450	3,600	11,050	13	1
XCG-9						23	0
XCG-10			7,980	8,000	15,980	28	0

	Wing			Weights		Troops*	Built
	Span (feet)	Area (sq. ft)	Empty	Cargo	Total		
XCG-10A	105	1,180	12,150	10,850	23,000	40	1
YCG-10A	105	1,180	12,150	10,850	23,000	40	6
XCG-11						28	0
XCG-12			9,349	8,282	17,631	28	0
XCG-13	86	873	7,000	8,000	15,000	28	2
YCG-13	86	873	7,000	8,000	15,000	28	2
YCG-13A	86	873	7,000	8,000	15,000	28	3
CG-13A	86	873	8,700	10,200	18,900	40	132
XCG-14	71.8	507	3,237	4,368	7,605	15	1
XCG-14A	71.8	507	7,500	8,000	15,500	24	1
XCG-15	62.1	623	4,000	4,000	8,000	13	1
XCG-15A	62.1	623	4,000	4,000	8,000	13	2
CG-15	62.1	623	4,000	4,000	8,000	13, 14	427
XCG-16	91.8	1,140	9,500	10,080	19,580	42	2
XCG-17	95	987	11,000	15,000	26,000	27	1
XCG-18A	71.8	507	8,000	8,000	16,000	30	1
XCG-19	85		6,380	8,000	14,380	38	0
XCG-20	110	880	24,000	16,000	40,000†	60	1
XFG-1	54	356	3,362	4,638	8,000		2
Assault Glider							
XAG-1					8,500		0
XAG-2					8,500		0
Navy-Marine							
XLRA-1	70.5	495	2,800			12	1
XLRA-2	70.5	495	2,800				1
XLRN-1	110	1,200	15,160	18,000	33,160‡	80	1
XLRQ-1	71	500	2,800			12	2
XLRG-1 (40 percent scale flight model)							1
XLRG-1	109		4,800			24	0
XLRH-1	110		4,800			24	0
Yugoslavia							
No designation				2,800		12	1

*For crew, see technical data.

† Although maximum take-off weight was 70,000 pounds, tow planes were not available that would tow a glider of this loaded weight. Thus, 40,000 pound limit was established.

‡ Overload weight was 40,000 pounds.

Powered Gliders

	Glider	Powered adaptation
Australia	DHA-G2	Glas II suction-wing
France	CM-10	CM 100
	CM-10	CM 101R jet
Germany	Go 244	Go 244
	Me 321	Me 322
Italy	AL-12P	P-512
Japan	Ku-7	Ki 105
Soviet Union	G-31	G-31 Yakov Alksnis
	BDP (S-1)	MP-1
	SAM-23	SAM-23
	IL-32	IL-34
United Kingdom	Hamilcar	Hamilcar X
	Horsa	Horsa
United States	CG-4A	XPG-1
	CG-4A	XPG-2
	GG-4A	XPG-2A
	CG-4A	PG-2A
	XCG-15A	XPG-3
	XCG-18A	C-122
	XCG-20	XC-123
	XCG-20	XC-123A

CG-4A Production Data

CG-4A Production Data to October 31, 1944		
Contractor	Average Cost	Delivered
Ford	14,891	2,418
Waco	19,367	999
Gibson	25,785	1,055
Commonwealth	24,232	950
Northwestern	24,543	887
G & A	25,144	464
General	31,010	1,013
Ridgefield	38,209	155
Robertson	39,027	147
Pratt, Read	30,802	925
Laister-Kauffmann	29,437	210
Cessna	30,324	750
Babcock	50,906	60
Timm	51,123	433
Ward	379,457	7
National	1,741,809	1

Horse-power Required for Operational Gliders at Sea-level

Glider Type	CG-15	CG-4A	CG-4A	CG-16	CG-13A	CG-13A	CG-10A	Two CG-4As Each	Horsa
Gross Weight	8,000 lb	7,500 lb	9,000 lb	19,500 lb	16,500 lb	18,580 lb	24,000 lb	7,500 lb	15,000 lb
Load	4,100 lb	3,600 lb	5,100 lb	10,080 lb	8,000 lb	10,080 lb	12,000 lb	7,200 lb	6,800 lb
Airspeed	H.P.	H.P.	H.P.	H.P.	H.P.	H.P.	H.P.	H.P.	H.P.
100	185	268	292	350	480	520	545	525	440
110	220	293	315	370	520	555	570	550	500
120	260	340	364	425	575	600	610	635	650
125	285	375	395	455	610	630	645	710	740
130	313	415	425	490	650	675	680	800	840
135	345	458	Max Speed	527	700	720	735	900	945
140	375 *·092	506 ·141		567	750	775	800	1000	1040
150	450	650		650	875	895	965	1150	1200

Note: *Data calculated by Glider Branch, Aircraft Laboratory from Wind Tunnel and/or Flight Test Data.*

Performance of the CG-4A in Approved
Tow-Plane Combinations (One CG-4A with cargo = 7,500lb)

Aircraft	One glider				Two gliders
	C-47	C-60	C-46	B-24	B-17
Ground roll (ft)	2550	1950	3300	3000	3,750
Distance to clear 50ft obstacle (ft)	3950	2950	5100	3750	5750
Climb (fpm)	275	600	275	530	300
Cruising speed (mph)	120	120	125	144	140
Range (miles)	830	990	950	1360	720

INDEX